"I highly recommend this amazing book. The Moseleys' concepts are new and revolutionary. They have changed me personally and have altered the way I work with my patients."

Jane Myers Drew, Ph.D.
Author, *Where Were You When I Needed You, Dad?*

"*DANCING IN THE DARK* is rare. The difficult and emotionally charged aspects of the shadow side of relationships are covered with clarity and thoroughness.

"Professional therapists and counselors as well as couples can use this book immediately. It cannot help but enrich the reader. I can easily recommend [it] to the professional and lay readership."

Harold D. Holder, Ph.D.
Director and Senior Scientist, Prevention Research Center

"This is a very hot book about a very hot, touchy, miserably frustrating, and crazy-making subject—relationships. Help is on the way! You've got to read this book!"

F. K. Heussenstamm, Ph.D.; Clinical Psychologist,

"Highest rating. Tone is warm, personal, and respectful of the reader. Very down-to-earth and easy to read, without offering quick fixes or oversimplifying the complexity of marital dynamics."

Daniel I. Malamud, Ph.D.; Therapist

"With *DANCING IN THE DARK,* one of the most effective teams for helping couples fall in love anew—though their relationships have become tortured or even dead—present for the first time the theory behind their powerful work."

David Feinstein, Ph.D.; Psychologist
Co-author, *Personal Mythology, Mental Acts*

"The work of Doug and Naomi Moseley offers a tremendous opportunity to delve into those areas of relationship that lie buried below the surface, waiting to sabotage our true longing. For those who seek a deeper and richer partnership, *DANCING IN THE DARK* illuminates many of these hidden patterns."

Ann Mortifee; author, singer, songwriter
1992 Recipient, The Order of Canada

DANCING
IN THE DARK

DANCING IN THE DARK

THE SHADOW SIDE OF INTIMATE RELATIONSHIPS

DOUGLAS & NAOMI MOSELEY

North Star Publications

Georgetown, Massachusetts

For permissions and reprint information,
contact North Star Publications.

ISBN: 1-880823-08-X
Library of Congress Catalog Card Number: 93-85994

First printing: 1994
Second printing: 1995

Cover design: Tamsen E. George
Editing/Layout: John Niendorff

North Star Publications
P.O. Box 10
Georgetown, MA 01833
(508) 352-9976
FAX (508) 352-5586

Printed in the United States of America

ACKNOWLEDGMENTS

Eva (diCasmirro) Babcock, for her insights, inspiration, and generous donations of time;

Catherine Jennings, Allan Paskow, Yolanda Stepien, and Leanne and Gary Cuddington, for adding their special ingredients to the mix;

Our editor, John Niendorff, for his competence, clarity, and composure;

Stephen Foster, for his valuable input;

George Trim, for taking a risk;

W. Brugh Joy, M.D., for providing a base for this particular broth;

All our friends and clients in Vancouver and Seattle, for offering us their vulnerability and their truth;

Alphonse Bouchard, for looking after so much of our physical environment this past year.

DEDICATION

In memory of Millie Botvinick and Jim Moseley.
With love to Elsa Moseley and Isadore Botvinick.

CONTENTS

CONTENTS

FOREWORD

This book is not intended for:

— anybody looking for a warm, cuddly book on relationship;

— people under thirty-five;

— couples in the romantic phase;

— anyone who has a desire to live only in "love" and "stardust";

— anyone looking for easy solutions or quick fixes;

— couples who don't know what it feels like to be "stuck";

— couples who are just trying to survive.

This book *is* intended for:

— couples who have chosen relationship as their pathway to increased consciousness;

— couples who want to get to the roots of difficult, recurring behavioral patterns;

— couples who recognize that successful, passionate relating requires continual effort and discipline by both partners;

— individuals who have not been successful in sustaining a nourishing relationship and are ready to look inward for the reasons why.

PREFACE

What's Wrong?

The complaints Naomi and I hear from most couples are remarkably similar.

The woman says she is not being "met in her emotions." She might express it in different words but her essential message is that she feels starved in her relationship and doesn't know what to do about it. She feels either like a mother to her partner or like a daughter to him, and doesn't seem to find much room to be a full-fledged adult woman.

The man says he is confused by it all. His partner seems to be looking for a powerful man who is capable of supporting her. But at home, she wants to control and take over his space. She is demanding, and if he gave into everything she wanted, he would be consumed. Overwhelmed. She doesn't seem to enjoy him sexually, at least not consistently or as much as he would like. She says she wants "his emotions," but he doesn't understand what that means.

She generally has more clarity about what her needs are, though she doesn't know how to go about getting them met in her relationship. He is less able to articulate his needs and tends to define his relationship problems in terms of what she says and what she does or doesn't do.

She is angry and he wants peace. They both feel empty and "stuck." Something is missing and, in terms of finding their way toward a relationship that is consistently and mutually fulfilling, both are clearly dancing in the dark!

INTRODUCTION

From Doug

I was told of a simple man who had lived in the woods observing nature for a good part of his life. He said human beings must be the only animals that don't "train their pups." I was in a vulnerable state after the breakdown of my first marriage and those words made a strong impression on me. I looked at myself and realized that although I had cultivated a mask of competence, underneath the surface it was quite a different story. Inside of me was a person who felt out of place, who felt he hadn't received the initiation or training required to thrive in the complex, fast-paced culture we all live in. The stark reality was that this person within me was not equipped to deal with intimate relationship.

As I began to wake up to my own sense of inadequacy and powerlessness, I started taking deeper looks at myself and our culture as a whole. I began to see that, regardless of chronological age, most of us operate at least part of the time from a young, immature place within ourselves that is covered by a facade of "adulthood." This emotionally immature part might be well-disguised in the everyday world, but in intimate relationship, hiding it becomes impossible.

In relationship both partners want to believe they are powerful, competent "adults" who are moving into intimacy with each other, while the truth is that self-centered, demanding, needy, frightened, wounded, uninitiated "children" lurk just underneath the surface and are present along with those adults. Neither partner wants to acknowledge the existence of these immature parts and both engage in strategies to cover them over.

The problem is that genuine, sustained intimacy thrives on truth. When two partners attempt only to show the "acceptable" parts of themselves and refuse to show their immature aspects (whether by conscious design or lack of self-awareness), they are not in truth. When partners are not genuine, the intimacy between them can't be genuine.

Recognizing that an immature "child" exists within each of us can be a painful and humiliating discovery. Most of us are disinclined to acknowledge this truth about ourselves. Yet the refusal to traverse this difficult territory in our inner being virtually precludes movement toward deeper awareness of self, and thus toward deeper levels of intimacy. Individuals who refuse to come to terms with these difficult inner parts become increasingly contracted and closed as they continue striving to sustain their "adult" image to intimate partners—who can't be fooled.

I love the wonderful richness, complexity, and mystery of intimate relationship. It has provided the crucible for most of my major discoveries about life and love. At the same time I have learned that passionate relationship does not just arrive by magic (as the child within me might wish). It requires preparation, diligence, instruction, rational understanding, access to feelings, and a willingness to look at parts of myself I don't want to see.

As a "pup" I didn't receive this type of training and instruction. I needed someone to alert me to the complexities of male/female relating patterns. I needed to know that passion can't be sustained without personal awareness. I needed a step-by-step analytical manual to help get me started on the right track. Those needs provided the inspiration to write this book.

From Naomi

When we moved to our country home, the garden had been unattended for many years. It was covered over with extra growth and strangled by quack grass and weeds. I was overwhelmed and in tears about how I would go about uncovering it—to reach the soil in order to plant and cultivate new life. It felt like an impossible job. But, with determination and patience, I slowly cut and dug and pulled until I found the rich earth below. Today the garden is a delightful array of colors and textures of luscious fruits, flowers, and vegetables. Maintaining it still takes daily care and attention but nowhere near as much as when we first arrived.

A relationship and a garden are the same. When a relationship has been neglected for a number of years, finding the soil so new seeds can be planted presents a major challenge. But with the right blend of elements—touch, truth, expression of feelings—partners can begin to reap the benefits of their new attention and effort.

This book is a guide to beginning the cutting, the digging, and the pulling away of debris so a reader's garden/relationship can start to regenerate. It takes hard work and determination at first but as time goes on it becomes intriguing and fun. First the new growth, then the fruits and flowers begin to appear and life becomes juicy and delicious.

PART ONE

The Dance

1

MANY SELVES, MANY DANCES

Intimate relationship between two people can be likened to an exquisite dance. The partners are separate and together at the same time, expressing individually yet also interacting—influencing and affecting one another. At best, they are able to find the perfect blend of discipline and spontaneity, creating something that is greater than the mere combination of two separate persons.

The dance of intimate relationship is particularly complex and fascinating because both individuals are made up of numerous inner "selves." Thus, intimate relationship between a man and a woman is actually an intricate potpourri of many dances among these selves, all occurring at the same time. Some are obvious. For instance, there is the dance between the adult man and the adult woman. There is also the dance between two good friends. There is the dance of two seductive lovers.

Other dances are less apparent, sometimes even invisible, but no less profound. For example there are: the dance between two worthy opponents, competitors vying for control; the dance between the mother part of the woman and the son part of the man; the dance between the father part of the man and the daughter part of the woman. And on it goes.

If you are new to the idea that many aspects of self can live in any one particular person, we have included a brief explanation in Appendix A. For the moment, however, simply consider that within each of us there is:

— a part that loves
— a part that hates
— a part that is selfish
— a part that is altruistic
— a part that doesn't trust opposite sex
— a part that is accepting
— a part that wants power over the other person in a relationship
— a part that wants to turn over all the responsibility to the other person
— a part that feels inadequate in relation to the partner
— a part that feels better than the partner
— a part that would sacrifice everything for love
— a part that doesn't even want to be in relationship.

Both partners have all of these parts within them (along with many, many more) and each part may take turns playing a prominent role in the relationship dance at any given moment.

What both partners most desire is the juicy, passionate dance between the mature adult man and the mature adult woman who are moving together in ways that nourish and expand each other, as well as those around them. All too often, however, that dance recedes into the background as the relationship develops, and the less fulfilling "invisible dances"—such as those of "good friends," "mother-son," or "father-daughter"—become dominant. Neither participant wants things to be like that, yet their relationship seems to have evolved in such a way that they feel powerless to change the way things are.

Why do so many couples seem to create situations which, when viewed objectively, look more like relationships of parent to child, or of nonsexual friends to each other, than those of fully mature men and women? *Why*, in spite of their wishes otherwise, do so many partners in relationship gravitate toward dancing the roles of caring brother and sister rather than those of passionate adults? *Why*, after the romantic stage, do intimate dancers have such a strong tendency to struggle for control rather than combining their energies into a fluid movement where power and control are shared equally?

Naomi and I believe the answers to these questions cannot be uncovered until the partners, individually and together, are willing to take an honest look at their most difficult aspects, those aspects to which we refer collectively as *the dark side*. A simple way to define "dark" in the present context is this: it refers to the many things we don't want to see in ourselves and our partners. The dark side includes hate, envy, greed, hunger for power, the capacity to use and abuse others—and all other aspects of the human condition that are offensive and are not enhancing to the ego. One feature of these aspects is that they are almost always more visible in others than they are in ourselves.

Most of us don't feel safe when confronted with these darker aspects—the shadow side—of human nature, especially when they pop up in our own lives. We tend to want to keep them out of sight. Therefore, whether by deliberate, conscious intent or unconscious denial and repression, dark aspects and feelings get covered over or disguised in favor of *masks* that are regarded as more acceptable. Thus, the "good girl" and the "nice guy"—two of the most widespread and typical masks—are created.

One of the main premises of this book is that masks, particularly those which are developed and held in place *unconsciously*, inhibit the evolution of deeper intimacy in a relationship. Two individuals living behind masks can only go so far with one another. Learning to be loving helps a relationship advance to a certain point, but partners who present masks to each other and attempt to be *only* loving sooner or later find

5

themselves bound up in resentments and a stifled existence. In our view, deeper levels of intimacy and love can only be attained by partners who are willing to be honest enough and vulnerable enough to experience together the full ranges of the human condition. But doing so—bringing conscious awareness to the invisible dances in relationship and exploring the darker aspects that exist behind the outer mask—is a complex and challenging task.

Much of what Naomi and I discuss in this book is easily demonstrated in real life, but writing it out is as challenging as trying to describe a physical dance with words. When we first conceived this project, we decided we could address that difficulty most successfully by using incidents from our own evolving relationship along with a liberal sprinkling of case examples of typical couples we have worked with. The development of the book would parallel our own learnings, particularly those that came after the romantic stage began to wane. We would explore the most typical relationship problems layer by layer, just as we uncovered those layers in ourselves and our own relationship. In other words, we would begin by talking about issues as they typically appear on the surface and then take a number of "passes" through them, each time attempting to explore deeper layers.

We decided to minimize the jargon of therapy, though avoiding it altogether proved to be impossible. Please don't get stuck if some of our concepts and vocabulary are not absolutely clear to you in the first pages. The terms will come clear as they are repeated in various ways and contexts. Small truths will add up to a larger picture as you go along.

Also, some of the material in this book is challenging and might be regarded as contentious. Since the later chapters depend on the foundation of the earlier material, we strongly suggest that the reader start at the beginning and go through the chapters in sequence in order to gain the fullest appreciation of the whole picture. Stay with it and we promise you that the dances which emerge will be exquisite, complex, and challenging.

PERSONAL HISTORY: A BIT ABOUT US

It seems to us that a Couple's Manual ought to say something about the authors' own relationship and how they arrived at the point of presenting their particular prescriptions for a passionate relationship. So, before we dive into the text, we want to tell you a little bit about us.

Our Present Marriage

We met in 1986, at a workshop in California. We both came into this relationship with a great deal of caution. The wounds from the breakdown of my previous marriage were still fresh. Naomi had been married twice before and was left with major questions about her suitability for married life. She was forty-one and I was thirty-eight. Like many individuals approaching midlife, we were so battle-scarred and so well-defended intellectually that unbridled passion and sustained intimacy seemed improbable—even though it is what we most wanted.

Fortunately, our emotions overruled our intellect and we had the great good fortune to experience almost a complete year of romantic love. We were at a stage in our lives where we both had very little in the way of worldly obligations. Naomi had sold her fitness business in Michigan a year before and was completing training in Gestalt therapy. I was taking a break from work I had been doing in the Canadian Arctic. Thus, temporarily free of the pressures and stresses of everyday life in our familiar routines, we devoted a good part of our energy to nourishing, observing, therapizing, healing, and treasuring each other.

We were almost opposites in personality (Canadian prairie boy meets Jewish-American princess). Like most couples in the romantic phase, we entered into relationship with the feeling that the power of unity and love could resolve all of our differences. We both wanted to believe we had transcended the problems that led to the breakdowns in our previous marriages. We came together with the hope that we had shed the dysfunctional aspects of our lives—as personified by our previous partners! We combined our energies without reservation and the power that came through this unification brought us to the edge of the mystical at times. We both felt very special—individually and as a unit.

For a good part of our first year together, we travelled, driving and flying to places in North and South America neither of us had visited before. Alas, however, the time came when we needed to settle down in one spot and make some money. As we began experiencing a more ordinary existence, our individual differences began to emerge. We got into major fights and, at times, felt as though the flow of love-energy that existed on almost a continuous basis in the early stages would never start again. Ironically, the aspects of ourselves that had been most attractive to each other became the things that were most problematic. (We'll offer more about that later.)

Though Naomi seemed to be totally different from my first wife and I appeared to be very unlike her previous partners, over time we began to see that the same kinds of issues and patterns of behavior were emerging in this relationship that arose in our previous marriages. Some patterns, in fact, were *identical* and I found myself acting out the same roles I acted out with my first wife. At other times I found myself acting out the roles my first wife used to play, while Naomi played *my* old roles. The patterns of behavior were still essentially the same; only the players had switched.

Sex, money, and children seem to be the major issues of contention in any intimate relationship. It didn't take us long to discover that our major quarrels would be over money. Neither of us was prepared for the intensity of the struggles that emerged in this arena, since, in our first marriages, money issues had been relatively easy to handle, with sex the major area of discontent.

A big part of our problem was that Naomi entered the relationship with significantly more money than I had. She was able to get along by spending her interest income and had difficulty relating to the anxiety I felt when I used my reserves. Since our intention was to share expenses equally and fairly, I usually wanted to spend less than she wanted to. She felt controlled. The times I was inclined to spend more, she would question whether I could afford it. I felt resentment. Yet these were only the surface expressions of deeper issues.

The partner who has more money usually seems to have more control and I didn't want her to have control. We started experiencing all-out fights over control and the situation evolved to the point where, for a period of months, the slightest issue could set us off. Neither of us was happy about this and it reached the point where our relationship was stretched to the limit of our mutual tolerance.

Fortunately, our sexual experience together proved to be enduring. Instead of abandoning each other, we stayed with the relationship long enough to recognize that our control issues also had deeper roots. If we were going to get anywhere, we needed to come to terms with what was happening under the surface.

One of the turning points came when Naomi and I went to see a therapist. After about twenty minutes of listening to our heated exchanges over money, the therapist remarked that we reminded him of a couple of three-year-olds in a sandbox fighting over a pail and shovel! We were both shocked and yet couldn't help chuckling at the truth of it.

That sandbox analogy inspired us to learn more about what was really happening with us. We eventually discovered that underneath the surface were two very frightened and angry "children" who didn't feel there was enough to go around, each of whom wanted to be taken care of by the other. Neither of these children felt very powerful in the world and, when the chips were down, both preferred security to love. These internal children were very afraid of being abandoned or used.

To add to the confusion, within each of us were also two *other* children, egocentric ones, who wanted every bit of the money and power for themselves! With all of these inner children in competition with each other, any issue could turn into a major struggle. Even a hint of surrender was out of the question.

In most areas of our lives we were able to maintain our adult masks, our facades, but when we dealt with such essentials as money, security, and control, our hidden, emotionally young child-parts came out in full force. We were able to disguise these internal characters during the romantic phase, but our having pretended to each other (and ourselves) that they didn't exist didn't eliminate them. As we spent more time together, the childlike parts began to surface—as they always do. We were faced with the choice of acknowledging these parts within ourselves and beginning to deal with them head-on, or continuing with our protracted, confusing arguments about who was right or who was dysfunctional in regard to money.

We gradually began to back away from our fierce attempts to prove our respective points (i.e., to gain control) and, instead, allowed ourselves to be vulnerable enough to expose our immature child parts. As we did this, we finally started to make some real progress in our struggles over money. We realized that no amount of arguing about the surface issues would have led to any lasting resolution of the deeper problems underneath.

As we became more conscious of these immature inner parts, another unsettling, evolving aspect of our relationship became more evident. Over time I realized I was acting less like an adult man and more like a son who was dealing with his controlling mother. It wasn't just a one-sided process, either, because she was acting more like a mother. As she did so, I adopted even more of what I now see were "son" ways of being. We became locked into dysfunctional patterns of behavior around these roles.

(I now describe the patterns in the past tense, but even these days, when we "forget to remember," they're there, staring us in the face. Powerful patterns of behavior, we have realized, are always ready to pop out and take over. All that's required is a certain voice tone or the raise of an eyebrow.)

Interestingly, as we slowly began coming to terms with the mother-son patterning which was apparent on the surface of our relationship, we developed more awareness about the ways Naomi felt like a daughter in regard to my critical, judgmental father aspect. In other words, below the mother-son drama was a hidden father-daughter component of our relationship, which was every bit as potent as the mother-son aspect.

In addition to examining ourselves, we began to study other partners in relationship and to ask questions. What motivates them? What are their conscious feelings? What are their hidden feelings? What are their attitudes toward life? What are their essential needs? What strategies do they use to get their needs met? What are their deeper feelings about the opposite sex? How is control related to personality patterning? What are the main patterns of behavior that women act out and what are those that men act out? What makes them want to stay together?

As with most men, my personal approach was mainly to strive for rational, intellectual understanding. However, after the experiences I've had in recent years, I must admit that intellectual understanding usually falls short of the mark when one is dealing with deeper issues of the human drama.

I came to realize that, to get to the real truth of what was going on at any particular moment, I needed to know my feelings a lot better. I saw the degree to which I could use rational understanding to fog over personal matters rather than to bring light to them. When it's used in that way, rational understanding can become part of a person's psychological defense system. Intellectualization gets used to analyze the other person's position or to prove a point rather than to develop genuine understanding of what is really going on within.

Naomi, on the other hand, tends to be attuned directly and immediately to feeling-tones and subtleties. She has the gift of being able to translate rational assertions into feeling-based words. She can listen to an individual's intellectual description of an issue and, without a moment's hesitation, identify the currents of feeling underneath the surface.

Not too long into our relationship, she began attempting to penetrate my intellectual beliefs—which often meant "my defenses"—and pressure me to look at feelings I had covered over. Unfortunately for me (but, in truth, fortunately), she could often *feel* faster than I could *think*, and my intellectual defenses were rendered impotent. Many of those times I resented her insights but, at the same time, a part of me appreciated hearing a deeper truth than I was able to discern through my intellectual analysis.

Thus, she and I bring those complementary perspectives to the writing of this book. In fact, however, only one person at a time can sit at a keyboard and actually put the words on paper, and my nature equips me for that task. But this book is, in every way, a collaborative work, representing Naomi's understanding as well as my own, presenting viewpoints we have come to share.

Two years after we got married, we decided to expand the counseling practice we had established and include couples. Couples seemed to sense greater safety working with a man and a woman. The men appreciated my rational interpretations and the women loved the way Naomi went straight for the feelings. As couples felt safer to open up, they regularly gave us the gift of exposing their deeper vulnerabilities.

As our couples' practice expanded, we soon began to see similar essential dramas or patterns of behavior among our clients—similar, in fact, to the patterns in our own relationship! These behavior patterns are discussed thoroughly in chapters 5, 6, and 7. As you will discover, we attempt a rational understanding *and* we attempt to trace the underlying feelings that accompany them. Our experience has been that when awareness is brought to these patterns in such a way, couples can begin to change how they relate to one another. The patterns themselves don't necessarily change, but the couples move from the frustrating place of "not knowing" or of "being confused" to a place of understanding some of the things that happen in their relationship. Once intimate partners begin to become aware of their own patterns, blaming each other for breakdowns in the relationship becomes increasingly difficult. Instead of using their energies to fight these patterns (and each other), couples are able to work together to become more conscious and aware. A behavior pattern is not as binding when both partners have awareness of who they are and what they are feeling.

The material in chapters 8, 9, and 10 uses these ideas to explore typical relationship issues in ways that are different, challenging, and evocative. In particular, we look at *control/power struggles*, the *arrival of children*, and *sexuality*. The insights presented in these chapters have proven to be helpful to many of the couples we see. At the very least, they are challenged to become more aware of who they are and what they are doing with each other.

We close our journey together with an exploration of *anger* in relationship. Naomi and I present this topic last because it deserves to be left ringing in the ears of the reader and because, after individuals have achieved more awareness about their feelings and their roles in the relationship, finding constructive ways to express anger opens a doorway to deeper intimacy and a more passionate life.

The inspiration to learn to deal with anger comes every day in our experience with couples. Over and over I have witnessed positive effects when long-held anger is expressed by one partner (and consciously received by the other). I realize now that when anger is held, intimacy cannot thrive. Partners who try *only* to be loving toward one another sooner or later find themselves bound up in resentment and stifled sexuality.

Coming Up:

In the next section (chapters 2 through 4), we start our journey together by taking a sober look at romantic love. We focus on a few of the troublesome dynamics and feelings at play beneath surface appearances. Our starting this way might lead some readers to assume we are pessimistic or cynical about relationship. Actually, we feel exactly the opposite. But our experience has been that, just as a tree needs to be pruned in order to grow into its true potential, excessive amounts of fluffy idealism need to be pared away if healthy growth in relationship is to occur.

PART TWO

The Shadow Side of Romantic Love

2

ROMANTIC LOVE UNCOVERED

He: Sure, I avoid some things in our relationship. I've been thinking of bringing them up, but generally everything is going well. And I hate to risk jeopardizing the great sex.

She: I want to change some things about him but I'm not saying anything right now. Later, when he's more committed, I'll feel safer expressing some of my discontent about who he is and what he does.

Welcome to the beginning of the end of the romantic stage! Masks are beginning to crystallize. Both partners have agendas they are not exposing; both have thoughts and feelings they avoid discussing. They do so with the intention of preserving the best parts of the relationship, yet as they avoid things, the relationship begins to deaden. As they withhold from each other, the fire of the relationship is beginning to be snuffed out. Unless they wake up and express themselves more honestly, what they are trying to keep from happening is what is going to happen.

Romantic Love

Romantic love is one of those characteristics of the human condition that almost everyone knows about and everyone would define differently. It is a stage of development that sets the foundation for a more enduring love. It is an ecstatic feeling that lasts only fleetingly, yet teaches us about passion. It is genuine love that makes a deep impression. It's a delusionary state that thrives on newness and lack of maturity. It is the dance of two seducers who have implicitly agreed to see each other as special and flawless for a period of time.

Each of these views offers some truth and yet none by itself can capture the full experience. But each does make clear the fact that romantic love can be viewed in an affirmative, optimistic way or in a more objective, even harsh way. Using the affirmative, "lighter" definitions sounds nicer and more closely fits the ideal most of us would like to experience. However, the harsher, "darker" interpretations, though more difficult to digest, are impossible to ignore if we are going to reach a deeper understanding of romantic love and the impact it has on individuals in relationship.

Let's look at the lighter side of romantic love first. In the romantic stage of a relationship, two people are almost involuntarily drawn together and have an experience of wonder, magic, and passion. In the discovery of one another, they find themselves in an open, available, feeling state; the heart of each person is open to the other. It can be an exhilarating experience because, from this state of openness, their fuller energies and creative potentials are available—both individually and together. People in romantic love tend to see the best qualities of their partners and hold the highest view of them. They experience what appears to be unconditional love for each other and from each other. When it is happening, they wish it would last forever, and those who are truly in romantic love believe it will.

From what Naomi and I have witnessed in life, the stage of romantic love is a vital component in the development of a long-lasting, passionate relationship. Most of us need a "jolt" to move us from our everyday,

18

isolated existence into intimacy. In that everyday state, our instincts are to put the self first. Suspending our defended and self-protective ways in order to enter into intimacy with another is not an easy process. Romantic love can be likened to some exquisite form of temporary madness which allows us to be open in ways we ordinarily are not.

When I look at our marriage, for example, I marvel at how Naomi and I ever got together in the first place! Home for me was my native Canada; Naomi was American. She had been something of a socialite; I lived mostly in my car and much of my world could be transported in a duffel bag. Her religious, economic, and social heritage was totally different from mine. Had we met in the course of our everyday experience, we might have had a casual interest in one another at best.

The differences between us extend a long way past our differing lifestyles. Her personality is forceful and gregarious. My personality is more contracted and cautious. Feelings are most important to her; rationality is primary for me. I live in control; she thrives on spontaneity.

The intensity of romantic love had the capacity to override our everyday consciousness and transcend these differences. We were looking into each other's souls. From that place, all the differences seemed merely superficial ones that could easily be handled (at a later date!). We entered into an instinctual, mystical union with one another that captured our full attention. Even now, recalling and rekindling that state serves as a kind of fuel which helps us stay together during the more difficult times.

Romantic love can be a wonderful experience, but couples who attempt to hold on to it too long invariably find themselves getting into difficulties. These couples usually fail to see that romantic love has an underbelly that needs to be recognized and acknowledged. For one thing romantic love is the domain of the emotionally immature child within us. This fresh, naive "child" wants to live happily in a state of unconditional love with an ideal partner. This child part doesn't want to deal with conflict, anger, power, rejection, or any of the dark parts that exist in all human beings. He or she does not want to recognize that a growing, stable, sustained relationship has a lot to do with learning about *conditional* love—with meeting expectations and demands.

The emotional children within all people desperately want to believe a good and loving prince or princess will come along and put them at the very top of his or her priorities. Almost every day in our counseling practice, we see women who are looking for the romantic, handsome, strong, feeling man capable of supporting them in every way. And there is no shortage of men who are looking for a beautiful, nurturing, accepting woman who thinks the same way they do.

Romantic love is the domain of the addict, as well. In our culture, we have become addicted to the image of romantic love. Instead of recognizing it as a starting place from which to move gradually into deeper possibilities and awareness, we attempt to hold on to it and perpetuate the "high." Just as addicts use a substance or a behavior to numb themselves to their inner feelings, people addicted to romantic love use it to avoid facing the truth of how they feel inside.

Romantic love also has a strong appeal for individuals who want to "live only in light and love." Whether they are simply attempting to create an ideal personal environment or have aligned themselves with a spiritual tradition which encourages them to transcend the "lower" parts of life, these types of people have difficulty tolerating the darker sides of the human condition. They also are likely to have difficulty sustaining a mutually fulfilling intimate relationship!

Naomi and I hold a pragmatic view. Romantic love, far from being an end in itself, stems from *a deep urge to become aware of who we are* in all of our complex and fascinating dimensions. We are instinctively drawn to a particular person who can help us in this life task more effectively than anyone else. In the early stages, we welcome the lessons this partner offers us about who we are; he or she tends to support the views we want to hold of ourselves. As time goes by, the lessons become more difficult. We are challenged to go behind the masks we habitually put on and take a look at our own patterns in clear, stark detail. Romantic love sets the stage for intimacy but the transition to deeper, more fulfilling love is accomplished only by those who are able to move on and to incorporate their darker aspects.

The "Dark Side": What It Is and Why It's Important

The great Swiss psychiatrist Carl Jung said, "One does not become enlightened by imagining light but by making the darkness conscious." These few famous words capture an essential truth that every couple would do well to remember. One cannot grow and expand (and thus live with passion and aliveness) without being prepared to incorporate the full range of the human repertoire—which includes the dark or shadow aspects of self.

When Naomi and I talk about "exploring the dark side" in regard to individuals in relationship, we mean looking at the aspects of being human that are not enhancing to the ego's view of the self. We mean looking at motivations based, in general, on selfishness, greed, arrogance, pride, and desires for power and control over others. We mean looking at aspects of ourselves we don't normally see or even want to see—for example the user/abuser, the angry bitch/bastard,* the judge, the victimizer, the controller, the person who wants to punish and dominate, and so forth. We also mean examining feelings that are part of the dark side, including anger, fear, hatred, jealousy, arrogance, and superiority.

---

* These are strong colloquial terms and could be easily interpreted as pejoratives, but they are not intended to denote anything unflattering about either of the sexes. We use these labels because powerful subpersonalities need powerful words and we couldn't find better ones to get the point across. Every woman has a "bitch" component and every man has a "bastard" component, and everyone who has been in an intimate relationship is well-acquainted with this fact. Nothing is inherently wrong with the bitch part of a woman or the bastard part of a man. If we can suspend our judgments for a moment, we discover that all subpersonalities contribute something to the human drama.

Jung also wrote about the unpopularity of working with darkside material. It is not an easy task and individuals in our culture get very little training in this area. In the earlier stages of socialization, we are taught that we ought to heighten the light or positive (though not too much!) and try to expunge, suppress, or at least ignore the dark aspects of our being. Individuals who do not control and mask their dark side often end up alone or at least out of the mainstream. And, during our early adult phase, when we are staking a claim for ourselves in the world, a "socially acceptable" personality is generally useful and even necessary.

Thus, for the most part, working with shadow material is a task best suited to the second half of life. In the first half, wanting to bypass or circumvent the darker, more difficult dimensions of self is natural and probably healthy. The younger mind likes to think all facets of self (and life) can be controlled. Qualities deemed desirable ought to be incorporated and heightened while qualities judged to be unacceptable ought to be eliminated. The rational mind in this stage believes unacceptable feelings can simply be eradicated by not paying attention to them or willing them to depart. ("I don't get angry; I'm a nice guy!" or "I'm a spiritual being filled only with love!")

Life, however, is never that simple; what works adequately at one stage in life frequently is noxious in the next. By midlife we begin to realize, if we are willing to look, that these darker feelings and aspects of self didn't just disappear. The human psyche, with all its richness and complexity, is not like a physical organism from which parts can be surgically removed and thereby rendered harmless once and for all. Developing an attractive personality *does not eliminate* the parts of ourselves that are unacceptable; they just become disguised or layered over. Furthermore, we cannot push those parts of ourselves away without paying a price.

People who are only willing to look at or to be aware of one portion of themselves are essentially living in a delusion—well-intended though that delusion might be. Behind their masks, they don't know who they are or what they feel. The control they exert to present an acceptable self-image to others (and themselves) is likely to leave them numb and without passion. Major dimensions within the self are lost or repressed. Living behind a mask takes energy. The process of suppressing becomes so habitual that they forget how much energy is consumed by putting on a good, pleasant face and living up to an image. When confronted by an unrelenting obligation to live up to an image, they eventually feel anger and rage—but even the anger needs to be pushed down.

Suppressing aspects of the self takes energy that could be used in more creative ways. In other words, people who refuse to come to terms with their shadow counterparts are destined to live out a contracted existence, behind a mask. Perhaps they will live the life of the "seducer," only showing aspects of themselves calculated to influence others. Perhaps they will end up living the life of the "good boy" or "good girl." Or perhaps they will just retreat into isolation and refuse to show any authentic parts of themselves to anybody. Any way you look at it, people who refuse to acknowledge their darker parts cannot live up to their full potential as human beings, let alone function well in relationship.

The truth is that few situations in life are better designed to bring out the dark, difficult aspects of the self than a sustained intimate relationship! Being human means having anger, self-centeredness, desire for power, desire for control, the urge to dominate, and so forth. In addition, we all have deep, complex, unresolved, feelings toward the opposite sex—feelings that are definitely not always enhancing to our self-image!

Of course, seeing a partner's "stuff"—his or her shadow side—is much easier than seeing our own. After a period of time, we are disappointed to learn that our partner is not all we had believed. We see clearly that he or she has been behind a mask, hiding or disguising aspects that might not be enhancing to an intimate relationship. We've been tricked!

Among other things, we discover we're with a person who, behind the mask, has a part that is very young emotionally and doesn't want to know about it. We're with a partner who wants to control us and make us into someone else (more like he or she is). We're with a partner who wants to stay blameless and *point the finger at us* for being infantile, controlling, and unaccepting. Many couples cannot cope with the discovery of these parts and split apart to search again for another partner who is "healthier."

By midlife, with a few relationships under our belt, we begin to make an amazing discovery. The same "faulty" partners emerge before our eyes each time we get a little deeper into a relationship. We are left either to renew the defending-blaming-justifying process in more sophisticated ways or come to terms with the realization that we need to dig deeper into ourselves to get to the root of the problem.

We attract partners who have the same level of awareness (and delusion) we do. Our partner offers us the gift—this profound gift—of letting us see who we are, warts and all. Judging from the failure rate of marriages, Naomi and I suspect that a large number of individuals prefer to decline the gift!

THE DILEMMA OF REVEALING THE DARK SIDE

We have already seen that during the romantic phase, the couple starts off fresh. The loving and giving parts come through. Both individuals want to see the best in each other. At the same time, their habitual suppression or repression of their shadow sides leaves them partially crippled and unauthentic. In this situation, intimate relationship will eventually break down.

In order to highlight this dilemma, let's take a brief look at a typical circumstance. All men and all women have somewhere inside of themselves a part we have called the good boy and good girl. What happens to these characters in relationship?

The Good Boy and Good Girl in Relationship

On the surface, the "good girl" (the nice girl) is friendly, accommodating, and helpful. Similarly, the "good boy" (or nice guy) shows friendliness, charm, and willingness to be supportive. They both got through the first part of their lives by being "good." It seems self-evident to them that by being good, they will attract intimacy. In the early romantic phase, things often do go well for the good girl and the good boy. They generally can attract partners and, once in relationship, they know how to please. After a while, however, the problems begin to emerge.

First, we'll examine how the individuals are personally limited by the role they have adopted. Second, we'll look at the consequences of living with a good boy or good girl.

Every woman, somewhere inside of her, has an "angry bitch" part who wants total control and is capable of destroying anything in sight. In the mind of the good girl, this angry bitch is not a part of herself she wants to accept. Perhaps it reminds her too much of her mother, and she is determined not to be like her! She also believes that if she did risk exposing this part, especially to someone new in her life, she could be rejected. As she (the good-girl part of her) sees it, the only viable choice is to mask over this part.

By hiding this bitch aspect, the good girl essentially creates a handicapped position for herself. She must live a false existence, always on guard to hide the parts she doesn't want to show. Feeling as though she needs to live a false existence in order to sustain a relationship, she eventually reaches a point of deep loneliness—despairing of ever truly being accepted for who she is.

At times, anger is appropriate and even necessary. The good girl, who cannot access her anger when doing so is appropriate, finds herself powerless in many of life's situations. She needs to resort to less direct strategies to have a sense of power and get her needs met. The woman who uses indirect ways to get her needs met is felt by others as being manipulative. The woman who feels constrained, lonely, and powerless and who acts in manipulative ways will have some difficulty sustaining a nourishing intimate relationship.

Much the same process happens for the "good boy." Whether they show it or not, all men have a steely "judgmental bastard" part within, who has a callous disregard for others and would get great pleasure out of subjugating everything in sight. However, the good boy sees himself as sensitive, caring, and loving, and doesn't want to accept this cold, judgmental, aloof part.

Not accepting or not "owning" unenhancing or dark parts of himself also has major consequences for the good boy. For example, the good boy often has developed his mask in reaction to what he believes to be negative masculine stereotypes. He wants to be the opposite of those stereotypes. But his problem is that as he pushes those parts of himself away, he also loses connection with part of his deeper masculine self. A male who is disconnected from his deeper masculine nature feels lost and powerless underneath the surface. He doesn't want to feel the parts of himself he has pushed away, and he doesn't want to feel powerlessness, either. He gets stuck in a type of limbo, blocked from discovering who he really is. The man who doesn't know who he is and what he feels can only pose as a man.

A good boy who believes he *needs* to be a certain way to be accepted by women feels angry underneath his facade. Being the good boy, he doesn't want to experience his anger and thus pushes it away or denies it. It is definitely not a feeling with which he is comfortable; displaying anger himself means risking his cover as the good boy. Unfortunately, without anger, he doesn't have full access to the energy required to meet the demands of life. He certainly won't be able to meet the darker, angry parts of his partner (which ultimately leaves her feeling unaccepted and even angrier). He, too, operates from a manipulative perspective, which can be very frustrating to his partner. A man who is blocked from his anger, disconnected from his masculine, and acting in manipulative ways will experience difficulty sustaining a nourishing, mature relationship.

So the problem is clear. As we progress in relationship, the darker side comes out anyway. Ask any man who gets deeper into an ongoing relationship with a "good" girl and he will tell you he has a major controller on his hands. She may not express anger but she "emits" it in ways that are unmistakable. She might be nice to others, but in the relationship with him, she can be extremely critical. A good girl who is angry underneath eventually does very little to initiate sex and often ends up closed emotionally.

Ask any woman who gets deeply involved with a "good" boy and she'll tell you that behind that cherubic smile, he is judgmental, impersonal, frequently withdrawn, and often working hard to change her into someone else. He uses calm, nice-sounding, reasonable words as he attempts to control her emotions and keep himself in power over her. He's so closed and defended that he doesn't even know how angry he is. It's all the more frustrating for her because he seems to be so "nice," especially to other women.

Every couple faces a dilemma here. Do they hide parts of themselves and live behind a mask in order to maintain the status quo and a sense of security or do they allow exposure of their difficult parts and risk potential abandonment? Either way there are costs, and the individuals involved need to respond to this dilemma in a way that suits them best. The choice to mask darkside material seems like the easier option, but Naomi and I have found that the costs of this option over the long run are high. As partners refuse to go behind their masks in the presence of their intimates, the chances are that the relationship gets more and more stagnant, more and more resigned.

The paradox here is that a refusal to acknowledge the dark sides of self to an intimate partner is a refusal to be vulnerable. When an intimate partner refuses to be vulnerable, it is felt as a type of rejection. Partners see what's really happening in their mates and, though they might not be able to articulate it, know they are being deceived. Over and over again, Naomi and I have seen that partners who try to maintain the love and smiles on the surface eventually close off to each other emotionally.

What If Everyone Did It?

Most people in relationship, upon seeing the nature of the darkside problem we have described, can recognize some value in understanding it more deeply. Their inevitable next question, however, points to the true nature of the difficulty. Often it is phrased in this fashion: "What would happen if all people were free to expose and vent their dark side whenever they felt like it?" But that is really a disguised way of asking, "What would happen if *I* were free to expose and vent *my* darker aspects whenever I felt like it?" And this is usually another way of wondering, "What if I lost control of myself?" Life presents many delicious conundrums to those who are seeking greater awareness and this is surely one of them.

There is one thing we are clear about. Naomi and I are not suggesting that men and women go out of control, that they blindly unleash their dark side, either on partners or on the world at large. Our viewpoints are directed at people who are mature enough to know the difference between becoming conscious of their dark side and destructively acting it out.

For some strange reason, many people seem to hold the implicit belief that denying their shadow side is an appropriate strategy because becoming aware of or acknowledging its existence would necessitate their *doing* something with it. For example, a partner in relationship silently believes that if he or she were to fully acknowledge deep rage, something would have to *happen* with it. Someone would have to be hurt or punished, or something would have to be destroyed. Partners don't want to have to deal with the consequences of acting out this type of energy and thus justify their denial of it.

But there is a big difference between becoming aware of a dark aspect and acting it out. In fact, it is really the immature child inside who is afraid of being overwhelmed by these feelings and possibly losing control. Becoming aware (an adult process) contributes to greater consciousness. Acting out darkside material (most likely an immature child process) usually has to do with domination, control, and defense against deep feelings of impotence. There is also a big difference between containing a feeling (an adult process) and denying its existence (most likely an immature child process).

Perhaps we need to answer the foregoing question with another question: "What happens when people refuse to come to terms with their own dark side?" By midlife, individuals who refuse to recognize this part of themselves often display ever-increasing tendencies to blame others for the difficulties around them. They focus on the dark side of others and anything or anybody unfamiliar becomes increasingly threatening. In intimacy they have an unconscious tendency to sustain situations where partners act out their darker feelings for them (like the never-angry husband with the raging wife).

In extreme situations, individuals who refuse to acknowledge their dark feelings reach the point where they can't hold themselves *in* anymore and they blow *out* in ways that are harmful to those around them. The newspapers are filled with stories of "quiet" people who repress their anger and hatred only to lash out unexpectedly in ways that are inappropriate or destructive. In fact, it would seem that people who are unconscious of their dark side are potentially more dangerous than people who *are* conscious of it.

As with most of life's complex situations, there are no easy, clear-cut ways to deal with darkside aspects in intimate relationship. We do know that individuals who are unwilling to accept their shadow parts need to live in some form of denial about themselves and can never experience being accepted fully for who they are, because they refuse to show themselves fully *as* who they are. If a relationship is going to develop in an atmosphere of truth, wholeness, acceptance, and ultimately love, partners need to know themselves and each other in all their dimensions—even if some of those dimensions are difficult to digest.

Coming Up:

Partners experiencing the heights of romantic love are usually in some degree of *collusion*. For example, they often have a mutual, unspoken agreement to withhold anger and judgment. They attempt to preserve harmony by avoiding areas of potential conflict and/or competition. In the next chapters, Naomi and I will elaborate this collusion and work with a case example in order to better illustrate the points we want to make.

3

SECRET AGREEMENTS

Before the fall from the grace of the romantic stage, partners in relationship act in concert with one another, harmoniously cooperating to get their mutual needs met. They have a common goal: to be together in as deep a way as possible. Both desire to prolong the merged, selfless state and hold on to innocent love. From this perspective, the notion of conflicting self-interest is almost irrelevant.

If we were to look at the dark side of this process, we could say that both partners implicitly agree to suspend many aspects of themselves so the feelings of romantic love can be sustained. They are being swept away by the force of their experience. This involves their entering into a type of collusion with each other.

Both partners are silently agreeing not to conflict. Both agree not to bring out their personal power to compete with the other. Both agree to withhold their judgments about the other. For the most part, both agree to refrain from expressing emotions that might make the other uncomfortable.

Collusion to Avoid Conflict and Competition

As a relationship progresses and two individuals begin to "emerge from the merge," their differing wants and needs become more apparent. More situations arise where the individuals are going to choose themselves first. Compromise is possible up to a point, but a time comes when their needs will be in direct opposition. If both individuals continue to be honest with themselves, conflict and competition will arise over which one's needs will be met first.

The chances are that neither partner wants to expose a major interest in self. Neither one wants to jeopardize the romantic feelings by engaging in conflict. In order to avoid conflict, at least one of the partners begins to suppress or deny needs. This suppression might continue for a time without major consequence, but a person who continually suppresses his or her needs in order to avoid conflict and in order to keep a partner content is living behind a mask.

No partner will go on suppressing his or her needs in favor of the other for extended periods of time without paying a price. Partners who refuse to deal openly with conflict invariably get deeper and deeper into underlying power struggles with each other—often to the point where both are blocked from getting their needs met. (This material will be covered in more depth in chapter 8.)

Collusion to Withhold Anger

When needs and wants are thwarted, feelings of frustration arise. Beneath these feelings is anger. The chances are that neither romantic lover is comfortable with expressing anger in the best of circumstances. Now, confronted with the threat of losing the object of their love, the partners are even more reluctant to express the feelings of anger they have. These feelings of anger, building up over time and remaining unexpressed, ferment below the surface. They begin to affect the relationship in ways that are frequently beneath the conscious awareness of the partners.

When feelings of anger build and are not brought into the open in a clear way, the relationship inevitably begins to sour. Partners who refuse to express anger directly may sustain the facade with casual friends or on the job, but in close quarters with an intimate partner, the anger will always comes out in one way or another. They become moody, cranky, unpredictable, and/or incomprehensible to each other. They begin to make underhanded comments. These comments may come out as sarcasm or humor at the expense of the other. Perhaps sudden outbursts, out of proportion to the situation at hand, will erupt.

Partners who won't express anger directly will eventually use indirect, manipulative means to get their way. For example, an angry partner who won't express her anger openly will seek to punish her partner by rejecting or closing off to him. She won't be able to "find the time" for him.

Anger that doesn't come *out* eventually goes *in*. In extreme situations, where the expression of feelings is completely blocked in relationship, anger can be directed toward the self in the form of emotional and/or physical disorders. Naomi and I have witnessed numerous situations in which a partner actually seemed inwardly to choose death rather than to express the anger he was feeling deep down. (Anger in relationship will be covered more thoroughly in chapter 11.)

Collusion to Withhold Judgments

A milestone that often signals the end of the "pure" romantic stage is the emergence of the first judgment by one partner about the other. The romantic stage will generally survive some basic expression of differing wants and needs—especially if the resultant power struggle is out in the open and the partners have at least some capacity for expressing anger. The emergence of judgments, however, is the first signal that romantic lovers are beginning to risk a clearer and more realistic perception of a partner.

Choosing a case example from our practice to illustrate collusion in romantic love almost involves a contradiction in terms. Couples in romantic love do not seek out therapy! So, as an example, Naomi and I have selected a couple who had been together for three years. In many ways they were past the pure, naive, romantic phase, yet they demonstrated the type of denial typical of the romantic stage. The events described below occurred over the course of several sessions.

This case example, as with all the examples that follow in subsequent chapters, is based on actual situations we have worked with. Names and details have been changed as necessary to protect the identity of the individuals.

CASE EXAMPLE: Tom & Laura

This was a second marriage for both partners and each was determined to make this one work. In the first session, Tom and Laura showed affection for each other and talked frequently about their fulfilling sex life. They always referred to each other using terms of endearment like "honey" and "sweetie." They both proclaimed theirs to be a wonderful marriage, full of romantic love, declaring that they had come to therapy with no specific intent other than to "fine tune" their relationship.

As their story unfolded, however, we began to see that a lot was going on beneath what they were presenting on the surface. Laura was close to being a workaholic and complained about being tired a lot of the time. She was often too tired to have sex.

When observing their relationship, Naomi and I could see clearly that Tom didn't really listen to Laura when she talked. And when she let down her guard, Laura appeared to be quite sad. Our addressing these sensitive issues was difficult, because each time we touched on one, Tom and Laura responded with affirmations about how happy their relationship was and how accepting they were of each other.

We learned that Tom thought of himself as an entrepreneur, but moved from one project to another without ever quite following through to the point where it paid off. The first time we met, Laura would smile and nod supportively as Tom talked about his soon-to-be-successful projects. In subsequent sessions, however, Laura's smile became more of a grimace. Finally, in one of the sessions, Laura came out with how unsupported she felt and how frustrated she was that none of Tom's schemes ever seemed to pay off.

Tom was noticeably stung by Laura's comments. He sat back for a minute, took a big breath, and started in with how he noticed that Laura had been putting on extra weight and he was getting tired of hearing her talk about going on a diet and never following through; in fact, he was beginning to feel less sexually attracted to her.

Laura responded that she felt very unappreciated and hurt. If she was going to follow through with dieting and working out, she needed more time. She didn't have the time because she needed to work to bring in the money Tom wasn't earning.

Tom answered that if he was going to succeed at his projects, he needed to spend less time attending to her and doing the things she wanted done. This was followed by a torrent of charges and counter-charges—with Tom and Laura each blaming the other for the shortcomings in their relationship. The exchanges grew more heated as the anger they both had obviously been carrying for a long time came into the open.

After some of this anger was vented, both were a little more willing to explore the deeper issues. Laura eventually revealed that she was beginning to see how she judged Tom as a failure and was afraid that if she openly acknowledged it, the relationship would be over. Further, as more of the underlying material came to light, she realized she enjoyed earning more money than he did and a part of her wanted him to remain powerless.

Tom saw how he had been judging Laura as fat and had been equally afraid that if he brought his opinion into the open, the relationship would be over. He also was able to acknowledge how he subtly sabotaged Laura whenever she got on track with a diet, by encouraging her to eat "forbidden" foods. It was a way of keeping her feeling inadequate and powerless.

They listened to each other intently during these exchanges—more carefully, I suspect, than they had for a long time. There was a period of silence as they both digested this information. Laura broke the silence by pointing the finger at Tom and saying, "You're a failure." He picked up on it and responded with, "You're fat." It was a tense moment but, at the same time, all of us were unable to keep from laughing.

Though they were not particularly pleased to hear these judgments from each other, neither was surprised to learn that the other had been contemplating them for some time. At last they were hearing the truth from each other and it was actually a relief, even humorous. The thing they both feared the most was out in the open, and dealing with these issues in a more comprehensive way was now possible.

COMMENTARY: Laura & Tom

Let's be clear that Tom and Laura are a very typical, normal couple. They care deeply for one another. They also both have parts within themselves that are judgmental, angry, competitive, blaming, and power-hungry. Naomi and I find it difficult to imagine how intimate partners can expect to go deeper with each other if they continue to withhold these aspects of themselves from each other. Thus, Tom and Laura have reached a decision point that all couples in the romantic stage confront: do they try to hold on to the status quo or do they risk going deeper?

If they opt to withhold their darker thoughts (in this case, judgments) and feelings (anger), they might be able to sustain an image of harmony and security. The price they pay is their need to put on a false face and cover feelings. If they risk being in their truth, the ultimate possible price is the loss of the relationship—or at least of the reasonably harmonious relationship they have experienced to this point. They risk a "fall from grace." They risk retaliation. They risk being abandoned.

Some individuals might say Tom and Laura would have been better off to have kept their anger and judgments to themselves, that they should have continued to show "happy faces" to each other. Now that each is aware that the other holds these feelings and thoughts somewhere inside, things will never be the same. Now that Laura knows Tom is judging her body, she might have more difficulty letting go in bed with him. Now that Tom knows Laura sees him as a failure, he will be stuck with that image for all time. Their relationship will be forever changed. They have been betrayed by their rude, impolite, self-centered, unaccepting partner!

On the other hand, we can look at how their relationship was going as they tried to hold on to the romantic stage. Both Tom and Laura were avoiding facing up to themselves in areas that were important parts of who they are. Both were feeling stuck; resignation was creeping into their relationship. Instead of happy faces, they were beginning to show each other "frozen smiles."

In fact, one of the things Tom most feared facing in himself was being a failure. This fear went much farther back than his years with Laura. He had spent a lifetime denying this part of himself. He enrolled in many "power of positive thinking" courses. He tried numerous other avenues to get power—including a number of ill-fated, get-rich-quick schemes. Deep down, he felt that if he were ever to acknowledge to himself that he was a failure, devastation would follow. He would have no sense of meaning. The avoidance of being a failure was the major force motivating him.

The judgment delivered by his wife was one of the things he was most afraid of hearing. He had been trying hard to avoid failure, yet the more he denied it, the more of a failure he became. As the years went by, running away from it was taking ever-increasing amounts of his energy.

At the same time, Laura had been avoiding her own judgment about Tom's failure. But just because she didn't bring it out didn't mean she wasn't feeling it. Any reasonably sensitive person already "knows" a partner's feelings and judgments even though he or she might not be able to articulate them with precision. Below the surface, Tom sensed

Laura's judgment. She knew what he was fearing but avoided the topic. In other words, judgments affected their relationship even when they weren't expressed aloud. When Laura's judgment finally came into the open, instead of the huge collapse Tom was expecting, he actually felt relief to hear the truth.

Failure to accomplish things in the world wasn't such a big issue with Laura. Her rawest nerve had to do with body-image and how she condemned her own body. Over the years she had studied food and dieting with the vigor of a professional nutritionist. She tried every lose-weight-fast scheme on the market and even developed a few of her own. Deep down, she felt that if she were ever to acknowledge to herself that she was fat, it would feel like death. Avoiding being fat had been one of her prime motivations, a raison d'être in her life.

She didn't want to hear the judgment that was delivered by her husband. Nonetheless she already "knew" he quietly judged her; she knew he often monitored her eating. And he knew she was fearing his judgment. When it finally came into the open, she too felt relief.

Tom's sense of failure and Laura's negative body image are parts of themselves they need to come to terms with in a truthful way if they are ever to reach deeper levels of maturity, acceptance, and wholeness. The judgment about Laura's body may have been delivered by Tom but, on another level, he was only the messenger. He was saying out loud what Laura said to herself dozens of times each day—and had been telling herself long before Tom came into her life. His judgment was actually her judgment against herself. His lack of acceptance reflected her lack of acceptance of herself.

Clearly it goes the other way as well. The judgment about Tom's failure was spoken by Laura but she only touched a nerve that had been supersensitive all of his life. It was an issue he was trying to avoid but needed to meet head-on if he was going to come out from behind his mask and find himself. With their judgments out in the open, they both have a chance to look at where the problems really exist—within themselves.

Anger and resentment had been building inside both of them for a long time. While this anger was suppressed and withheld by each of them from the other, they both began to feel stuck and frustrated. Below the "sweetie" and "honey," they were both silently blaming the other for the deficiencies in their relationship. When the anger came into the open, there was more space for some fresh air, more opportunity to move out of the stuckness they were feeling. In fact, we learned later that Tom and Laura went home after the judgment session and had their best sex in years. It often happens that way: honesty releases energy.

From our case study, we see that Tom and Laura risked conflict and exposed the anger and judgment they had been holding in. Indeed, their doing so marked their "fall" from the grace of the romantic stage. At the same time, however, their relationship was enriched. The potential for growth, awareness, and deeper love was heightened.

Our experience is that when couples begin withholding from one another, regardless of whether the material they are withholding is positive or negative, problems begin to emerge. Sexual relating diminishes. Passion diminishes. At least one of the partners starts to feel deadened. In short, the relationship begins the journey toward stagnation. If it stagnates for too long and the partners refuse to deal with their truth, the relationship moves into deeper resignation; it starts to die, along with the individuals in it. Eventually it reaches a point of no return. "They died in their forties," someone once said, "and were buried in their eighties."

Coming Up:

On the surface, partners in the early stages of relationship see only the best qualities in one another. However, when a person idealizes another, he or she is not really seeing or accepting that person realistically and the consequences are profound. We'll be examining this phenomenon next.

4

THE ONE YOU ADORE IS NOT REALLY ME

When partners idealize one another, they may believe they are showing love; they are, after all, endeavoring to see the "best" (or what they judge as best) in the other person. Idealization has many of the same qualities as *unconditional love*, and when we are being idealized, we may seem finally to be receiving the unconditional love and acceptance we crave—or at least "craved" at the point in our lives where we last allowed ourselves to fully feel our true feelings. The behavior of someone exhibiting unconditional love is quite similar to that demonstrated by someone who is idealizing another; in the early stages of a relationship, confusing the two experiences is easy. As a relationship progresses, however, the differences become recognizable and are important to understand.

Unconditional love is one of the greatest gifts people can offer. It implies deep acceptance of another person's essence. Idealization has nothing to do with acceptance. Idealizers are seeing *what they want to see*—usually having to do with *their own* highest expectation of the person being idealized. Essentially, idealizers are seeing only a very limited vision of a person. As they hold on to this series of selective

41

perceptions, this ideal, they are seeing what is essentially an illusion of their own creation. Their sight has more to do with a perfected ideal than an ordinary flesh-and-blood person. Extreme idealizers (perhaps the ones who most strongly believe they are offering unconditional love) will often refuse to see anything other than their ideal.

Those who receive idealization typically enjoy it at first. Because they are being acknowledged as special, they seem, on the surface, to be receiving love. They feel honored. What could be better than having a partner who wants to, and does, always see the best in you?

But as time passes, people who are idealized begin to feel discomfort. On one hand, they enjoy the experience of being seen, acknowledged, perhaps even adored. On the other hand, they feel anger, disgust, and a tumult of similar difficult feelings that don't seem justified.

These latter feelings are important to recognize and understand. When people are only seen for their specialness and not accepted just as much for their ordinariness (which includes the shadow side), what they feel underneath the surface is rejection. When they feel rejected and defined by someone else's expectations, one of the major consequences is anger. But, as idealized individuals, they are not "expected" to have anger and they often push the anger out of their awareness.

This is all very confusing to intimate partners who are being idealized. They are adored and *feel* rejected. They are seen as powerful and yet they *feel* powerless. They are told they are special and yet they don't *feel* special. They are angry, but believe they are not *supposed* to be angry. Small wonder that idealized individuals often end up feeling confused and out of touch with themselves.

In order to understanding these ideas better, let's look at a case example.

CASE EXAMPLE: Maureen & Keith

Maureen and Keith had been married seven years. They came into therapy because she was threatening to leave him. On the outside they looked like the "perfect couple." He was a handsome, intelligent lawyer;

she was an attractive, feeling woman who developed a career for herself in the cosmetics industry.

Keith was a reluctant participant in the session and wouldn't have come in without Maureen's ultimatum. He made it clear at the beginning that he was suspicious of the therapeutic process in general and believed they ought to be able to "just work things out" on their own.

As Keith attempted to describe their situation from his view, he spoke glowingly of his partner. He described being "smitten" by Maureen from the beginning of the relationship. She was beautiful, intelligent, sexy, and had many talents. He went on to describe their courting days and how much fun they had. He was perplexed about why she would want to leave him and was unable to understand why they couldn't carry on as they had in the beginning. As far as he was concerned, she was still beautiful and perfect. He pointed out his belief that she got everything she wanted and was exaggerating their difficulties. In his view, they had a great relationship up until about a year ago, when she sought therapy.

Maureen had difficulty expressing the reasons for being dismayed by the relationship. The only way she could describe her problem was that she had reached the point where, most of the time, she wanted to push Keith away. At the same time, she didn't want to leave him and their comfortable existence. She agreed that at the beginning things went well, that they had a lot of fun together. His proclamations of love sounded good but she couldn't ignore her feelings that "things just weren't right." The previous year, these feelings had worsened to the point of her having intense depression, which led to her seeking personal therapy. Even in therapy, she found herself experiencing guilt for feeling so bad when she appeared to have so much.

As our session progressed, Keith showed himself to have great facility with words, and he told engaging stories. Before long, though, we noticed that he seldom said anything about his own feelings; everything seemed to orient around Maureen's actions and feelings. Every time we brought the focus back to his expressing what his feelings were, he was stumped. He would try for a sentence or two, then start off on another story and invariably swing the attention back to Maureen and her issues.

When we pressed him to describe his feelings, the best Keith could come up with was that he felt he was being controlled by Maureen. Throughout the entire session, he disclosed very little of a personal nature, and when we pointed this out, he said he could not understand what we meant; he thought he *was* sharing about himself. He felt "confused."

Though she seemed to be open to him at the beginning of the session (she was clearly excited that he agreed to come to therapy), she got colder toward him as time progressed. Keith kept a calm, collected face throughout the session. At the end, when questioned about her feelings, Maureen said she felt "sad," "alone," and "hopeless."

COMMENTARY: Keith & Maureen

A great deal more is going on in this relationship than idealization, but, for now, we'll just focus on that part.

Maureen found a man who idealized her. In the beginning she was happy. She liked being idealized and a part of her wanted to live up to his ideal. The problem was that, as the years went by, though she desired his continuing idealization, she began to feel angry, discouraged, and disgusted with him. Her logic told her she had no reason to experience these feelings. So, rather than openly acknowledging those feelings, she began to close herself off.

Keith liked to have everything on an "up" note; he wanted to see their relationship in a positive light. He was genuinely shocked that Maureen was threatening to break up with him. He still loved her and was sure something in *her* was leading to this breakdown. If she could just fix "her problem," then everything would return to the way it was during the earlier stages.

For Maureen: What Was Going on Below the Surface?

The person who accepts idealization is subject to the control of the idealizer. In order to live up to Keith's ideal vision of her, Maureen was continually dancing to his tune, attempting to be perfect. Relative to him, she felt powerless. Even though she desired his idealization, she began also to feel an obligation to live up to it. It doesn't take a genius to figure out what's going on inside of a person who feels controlled and under continued obligation to live up to another's image.

Idealizing a person is actually similar to judging that person, except the focus is on desirable qualities rather than undesirable ones. As the focus of Keith's idealization, Maureen felt she was continually being evaluated and assessed. In being the center of so much attention, she also became the focal point of anything that was not going right in the relationship. She felt she was being blamed for their problems (and she was), which made her even more angry.

As Keith steadfastly held on to his idealized vision of her, he was essentially attempting to sustain a relationship with a fantasy woman. He was seeing *what he wanted to see*, not necessarily who she was; in fact, he only wanted his fantasy woman (who would be much easier to deal with than any ordinary mortal). He built her up and told her things were going fine, but he was not seeing Maureen's ordinary flesh-and-blood woman, who—as she well knew—had many dark, imperfect aspects. In effect, he was denying those very real parts of her. As a woman, she felt rejection.

Individuals who are objectified in this way, especially by their intimate partner, are going to experience many such troublesome feelings. In addition to hurt, rejection, and anger, they usually end up scorning their idealizer for being so shallow, so unable to see what's really going on. When their mate steadfastly persists in seeing the ideal, people who are idealized can begin to question their own self-perceptions, even their own sanity.

The first problem for Maureen was that Keith's ideal woman "shouldn't have" any of these difficult feelings—especially in regard to him. Therefore, if she was going to continue attempting to be his perfect woman, she needed to swallow them. Furthermore, justifying her own upsetting feelings to herself was difficult for Maureen since, on the surface, she seemed to be dearly loved by him and to be getting what she wanted.

When a woman has no outlet for her feelings in a relationship, she will eventually close down, and if she closes down far enough, she feels sadness, depression, and hopelessness. Of course these difficult feelings wouldn't fit in with Keith's fantasy image, either! For a woman who is still trying to live up to the ideal, there seems to be no way out—except perhaps to find a way to end the relationship. Even though she didn't understand why, Maureen was at that point.

For Keith: What Was Going on Below the Surface?

Idealizers in relationship keep themselves in a position of power. By focusing on Maureen, Keith was implicitly able to hold her responsible for all that went wrong in the relationship. Furthermore, because no human being can live up to a myth, idealizers like Keith can always look at their partner as having fallen short of the mark.

He was not *consciously* trying to hold on to a power position in the relationship—in fact, the chances are that he would loudly proclaim he had Maureen's best interests at heart (and, in his own mind, he probably did). Keith was not aware that he was out of touch with himself, that he was trying to have a fantasy relationship with a fantasy woman, attempting to live a myth. He lived within the narrow egocentric limits of his own opinions, which kept him oblivious to and aloof from the difficult parts of his inner being.

As Keith continued to focus his idealization on Maureen, he was able to avoid looking at himself and thus avoid running the risk of exposing any vulnerability he might find. He was, in effect, hiding. Not only did that provide him with some safety, but it also gave him even more power in the relationship. While Maureen was busy attempting to live up to his image of her, she was much less likely to challenge him!

To avoid feelings of distress, a person who is uncomfortable around people of the opposite sex either avoids them or aspires for control. If Keith had allowed himself to be vulnerable and had exposed his feelings, he would, at least, have acknowledged that he felt uncomfortable around women who weren't busy trying to live up to his ideal. Had he been willing to go deeper into himself, he would have become aware of his desire for control in the relationship. However, Keith was in total denial of his "controller" and, as is typical of those who deny a shadow component of themselves, he could only see that *she* was trying to control *him*.

Idealizers need to make their partner special so they can feel special within themselves. Having an "ideal" partner helps them avoid their own inner sense of unworthiness and unimportance. But attempting to create a heightened image of self by idealizing another can only work for a limited time before the whole charade begins to break down. Sooner or later somebody begins to wake up to the absurdity of the situation.

Until Keith is willing to take a more honest look at his role in this breakdown, he will continue feeling "confused"—a word people often use when they're not fully in touch with their feelings.

Where Can Keith and Maureen Go Now?

All people need to be honored for their "ideal" parts *and* be seen and accepted for their dark, angry, difficult parts. They want to be idealized to some degree and also be seen and accepted for their imperfect, human selves—especially by their intimate partners. This couple has been living in the ideal for seven years; if they want to salvage their relationship, they need now to deal with things that are less than ideal.

In a way, Maureen's threat to end the relationship is really a challenge to Keith to get more in touch with, and ultimately to heal, major unseen problems in his deeper nature. Rather than spending his energy focusing on her "perfection" (and thus avoiding himself), Keith could start a journey into deeper awareness by allowing his feelings of unworthiness, neediness, powerlessness, and anger to surface.

If Keith is willing to allow some of these difficult feelings into his awareness and make an earnest attempt to find the truth of who he is behind his facade, the relationship may be healed. But this will be a tall order for him, particularly because his professional training (as an attorney) will actually get in his way. Individuals trained to use words and rational analysis always have a propensity to attempt to prove themselves right and not allow themselves to be personally vulnerable. Acknowledging his feelings of neediness and powerlessness is going to challenge the image, the mask, he has spent much of his life developing. With Maureen poised to leave after years of discontent, he may have to go through a second marriage and experience the threat of being rejected again before he becomes willing to wake up to his own role in the breakdown.

Let's be clear that Maureen has an equal role in all of this, since the idealizer needs to have someone who is willing to play the "idealizee." She, therefore, needs to get to know who she is behind *her* facade. If she is so willing (and so wanting) to turn over the definition of herself to someone else, she must feel tremendously unworthy. At the same time, she wouldn't be so caught by Keith's idealization if she didn't have a highly inflated view of herself. Maureen needs to wake up and "get a life."

Maureen and Keith could also benefit from understanding more about the invisible "dances" in which, beneath the surface of their awareness, they have been participating. That is what we will be examining in the next section.

PART THREE

The Impossible Search for the Perfect Partner

INTRODUCTION

The Invisible Dances

After the romantic ardor has cooled, the difficulties that emerge in relationship are predictable. Patterns of behavior appear with which neither partner is satisfied. Typically, one or both persons complain that the partner is closed and rejecting. Perhaps the partner is regarded as too needy, consuming, or controlling. Or the partner is not supportive enough. One or both may complain that the other is taking a "better-than" position. At least one has a nagging sense that a mistake may have been made, that the partner is not good enough or not growing fast enough.

Nothing really ever seems to change. They may talk of altering their behavior and occasionally resolve to do so, but a few weeks later the situation is the same again. Both partners feel "stuck" and "frustrated," yet cannot really understand what is going wrong.

Some aspects of the relationship do work, however, and the partners are reluctant to give up the positive aspects of being together. Each has a deep caring for the other but the passion between them has greatly diminished or disappeared altogether. They may have a good brother-sister relationship, but it clearly falls short in the man-woman dimensions.

When Naomi and I encounter these couples in counseling situations, we see, in at least one of the essential areas of relationship, whether it be money, sex, or children, that the partners are in competition. And while they may claim their relationship has become passionless, an outside observer sees clearly that they are passionately engaged in an invisible dance—the dance of power and control!

51

Upon closer examination, this observer will note that other precise yet invisible dances closely related to those of power and control are also going on under the surface. These are the dances in which the woman plays out the roles of mother and/or daughter while the man acts out the roles of father and/or son. These parent-child dances, fascinating to watch, are even more interesting because, while the partners are playing their roles with great gusto, both are usually oblivious to what they are doing! Among all of the invisible dances a couple will engage in, we believe the parent-child dances are the most important to understand, because the amount of dysfunction in a relationship usually seems directly related to how much time the couple spends involved with them.

Though the parent-child dance is more difficult and complex to describe than the dance for power and control, Naomi and I have decided to begin our exploration with it. Our experience has been that a much richer exploration of power and control is possible when the dance of mother-son and father-daughter is understood.

The next chapter of this section, chapter 5, will define concepts and give an overview of the parent-child dance. In chapter 6, we'll look at case histories that illustrate what we call mother-son relationships, where the woman's mother-aspect and the man's son-aspect seem to be the dominant roles in the relationship. In chapter 7, we'll examine father-daughter relationships, where the man's father-aspect and the woman's daughter-aspect appear to be more prominent. Finally, in chapter 8, we will examine how mother-son and father-daughter patterns fit together in an invisible dance for control.

NOTE

Throughout the following chapters, we frequently use the terms "child" partner (or type) and "parent" partner (or type). Neither of these terms is intended to be pejorative; both simply refer to subpersonalities all of us have and all of us encounter in relationship. These terms—as well as "mother," "father," "daughter," and "son"—are intended to describe *roles* played out by men and women in relationship. Although every person is capable of playing every role, certain types of individuals tend to fall more readily into a parent role and certain types tend to adopt a child role in relationship. But, as we shall see, both partners are capable of switching roles in the blink of an eye.

5

BONDING PATTERNS: THE INVISIBLE DANCE BETWEEN "PARENT" AND "CHILD"

How to Recognize the Presence of Bonding Patterns

Among the most frequent complaints we hear in our office is this: one partner is feeling disgusted at the prospect of spending a lifetime "being the parent" for the other. For example, a woman will talk about how frustrated she feels being with a "boy." She doesn't feel he has enough maturity to match her emotionally, especially in regard to anger. Whenever she expresses her emotions, he has a strong tendency either to withdraw or to close off altogether, like the young boy who tunes out his mother. Her partner is likely to be passive-aggressive or perhaps he tries to please her in ways that she feels are unauthentic. He may be unable to function well in the world outside the home and depend on her to do it for him. Perhaps he is too needy and clings to her. Whatever the circumstance, she feels he is demanding that she be a "good mother" to him, but *she doesn't want to be his mother!*

A man may come up with a variation of the same theme. His frustration often stems from being with a partner who doesn't seem to be able to match him in his sexuality. She won't initiate sex or, at least, doesn't consistently seem to enjoy him sexually. Her moods are incomprehensible. She frequently withdraws into herself and closes off to him. She wants emotional and material support from him but doesn't seem willing to or capable of offering the support he needs. There is no end to her demands that he do more for her, yet she doesn't appreciate what he is already doing to keep everything going. She is like a young girl who is looking for a "good father," but *he doesn't want to be her father!*

On the other side of these scenarios, the partner is repelled at the prospect of having a "parent" for a mate. For example, a man will complain about how controlling his partner is. She hangs over his shoulder, watching him all the time, looking to change him. She says she wants emotions, but when he presents her with feelings like anger, she tries to control them as well. Perhaps she says she wants him to be powerful, but in reality she seems to want to bring him down, to pull him away from situations where he does feel power. She finds fault with many of the tasks he takes on. She wants to cut him off from friends and activities she doesn't approve of. Though she appears to be "nice" on the surface, she is angry and critical much of the time. It's almost as though she needs to act like his mother, but *he doesn't want her to be his mother.*

A woman will complain about how dominating her partner is. He holds himself in a superior place and makes her feel small. Whenever she tries to gain some power, he wants to bring her down. On the surface, especially to the outer world, he might appear to be powerful, but to her he often feels like a "needy leech." She feels suffocated. She hates being treated as an underling. *She doesn't want him to be her father.*

What Do They Really Want?

After a couple has voiced a few of these grievances, we get around to asking the partners what they *do* want from each other in their relationship. The actual words vary according to their willingness to be direct, but the essential reply is the same. They want their partner to grow up—and treat them as they deserve to be treated. The woman wants to be adored by a man who is sensitive to her emotional needs. Her partner should grow up so she can experience being supported and cared for by a "real man." The man wants to be received and nurtured by a woman who is able to surrender and open to him. She should grow up and become a "real woman."

They both want their partner to stop attempting to control them—and preferably to offer unconditional acceptance instead. They want the partner to be there when they desire the partner to be, and to give them space when they want space. The partner should be open and vulnerable when appropriate, but not demanding or needy. The partner should recognize their needs, and fulfill them without having to be asked.

When the couple gets to the point of articulating these needs, wry smiles often emerge. They say they don't want to be a parent to their partner and they say they don't want their partner to be a parent for them. Yet, when asked what they desire in a partner, both come up with a description that is suspiciously similar to that of a child who is seeking an ideal parent.

From the eyes of the child within, the woman *is* seeking a good father. She is looking for a man who will accept her totally, support her when she wants it, adore her, attend to her feelings, and give her all the attention she needs. The man, in turn, *is* seeking a good mother, who will accept him totally, nurture and care for him, make sure his needs are met, and hold him in the special regard he thinks he really deserves.

Both partners are seeking an ideal "parent" yet they end up with a "child." Or they end up with a partner who reminds them all too much of the parent they *don't* want, a parent who is controlling, critical, and rejecting much of the time. It's a confusing situation and both partners will need to step back and look at what is really going on—particularly within themselves.

To get a better understanding of any complex situation, a model is helpful, and the most effective one we have found is that of *bonding patterns*. Like any model it has its limitations but our experience has been that it is the single most important concept to grasp if one wants to develop more awareness of the inner workings of intimate relationship. It forms the foundation of the material that follows in this book.

BONDING PATTERNS DEFINED

Naomi and I first heard the term "bonding pattern" on an audio tape by Hal Stone, Ph.D., who, along with his wife, Sidra Winkelman, Ph.D., has done some great, pioneering work in this area.[*] In a relationship between a man and a woman, a bonding pattern exists when the mother part of the woman connects with the son part of the man, or the father part of the man connects with the daughter part of the woman. While bonded together as mother-son or father-daughter, the partners do not relate to each other as conscious adults but rather as parent and child. In such a situation, it is almost impossible for both individuals to receive the nourishment that an intimate, truthful relationship between an emotionally mature man and an emotionally mature woman can provide.

In a healthy relationship, the woman occasionally mothers her partner in a nurturing, supportive way; this is balanced by the times when the man takes on a nurturing father role for her. In every relationship, parenting a partner who is in need may be appropriate and even necessary. This kind of parenting, when it occurs by choice and both parties are aware of what is happening, can be healing to both individuals.

However, a bonding pattern is not a healing experience—in fact, it is quite the opposite. When a couple is bonded together in such a way

---

[*] See their book *Embracing Each Other: Relationship as Teacher, Healer & Guide* (New World Library, San Rafael, CA. 1989).

that one partner habitually takes on the parent role in relation to the other's child role, it has little to do with conscious choice. Neither partner is happy about being locked into these roles; both feel constricted and angry.

The parent partner doesn't get nourished by being with a partner who is childlike and the child partner doesn't expand by being with a partner who is parent-like. This is a confusing situation for the participants because the pattern, once it is established, is so potent and so automatic that it is highly resistant to change. Partners find pulling out of the relationship difficult because the bonding effect is so strong. (Also, bonding patterns don't usually come into full bloom until a significant commitment has been made, when running away is harder.)

In order to understand this more clearly, let us sketch out the types.

Parent Type

Parent partners tend to adopt a role that involves being stable and responsible in the relationship. They may become a "good parent," who is benevolent and nurturing, or a "bad parent," who is strict, critical, and judgmental; most likely they are a combination of both. Though they may try to disguise it, they assume an attitude of the one who "knows better." Since money is a symbol of power, parent types like to keep control of finances in a relationship. They may moan about it later on, but parent types have an uncanny knack for attracting partners who eventually demonstrate qualities that are associated with the child type.

Child Type

Because of their tendency to be inconsistent and/or fearful, child types are likely to show some measure of powerlessness in coping with the world. Some will act out the "good child," who tries very hard to gain appreciation and acceptance through doing things perfectly. Others act out a "helpless child," who collapses in the face of responsibility. Another common role is that of the "stubborn, defiant child," who refuses to meet any demands that are made on him or her and has a tendency to respond by doing the opposite of what is being called for at the moment. Child types might hate it later on, but, mysteriously, they have a very strong tendency to choose a partner with parent qualities.

The Invisible Dance between Parent and Child Types

In the first stages of relationship, parent and child types often make a good fit. The child partner is attracted to the stability and responsibility the parent partner represents. The parent partner is drawn to the enthusiasm and energy of the child partner. The parent offers support; the child offers stimulation and fun. Frequently, the parent has more comfort in the material world, whereas the child is more oriented to creativity and fantasy. By combining their resources and teaching each other what they know, they could help each other to become more whole. However, without a deliberate intention by both partners to do so, matters seldom work that way and, over time, they begin to feel stifled by their roles.

Unless a significant age difference exists, parent-child dances may not be obvious at first. But, as time goes by and the commitment deepens, the roles become more evident. The partners taking the parent role can be identified by the way they achieve and hold on to power in the relationship. They speak with the voice of a parent, the one who knows. They point with the finger of a parent. They may openly criticize and judge or they may silently assume a "holier than thou" perspective. The parent partner accepts no blame.

Partners taking the child role can be identified by the way they reject attempts by the parent partner to dominate. Like an actual child, child types will, at different times, rebel, defy, or withdraw. In an intimate relationship, they will often hold on to their sense of power by habitually adopting defensive postures or by pulling away from their partner. They might physically depart or absent themselves emotionally; either has the same effect. If the child type is feeling totally powerless in the relationship, frequent retreats into depression are not unusual.

To get clearer on how this works, let us begin the analysis of the basic steps in the parent-child dances. We will get to the more complicated steps in the chapters that follow.

MOTHER-SON DANCE

In a mother-son relationship, the woman unconsciously adopts the role of parent. She becomes "mother." The man she is with, if he is not alert to what's going on in himself, will have a tendency to respond with "son" behavior. For example, if she acts out a critical mother, he might respond by closing off and becoming a sulking child. A demanding mother activates a rebellious son. If she is an indulgent mother, he will become irresponsible. There are no hard-and-fast rules here, but one thing is clear. *The more she acts out the mother role, the more he acts out the son.* He becomes the very thing she doesn't want him to be.

Looking at it from the other side, the man unconsciously falls into the role of son. He sulks or becomes secretive. He defies. He charms. He ignores and goes deaf. He pleases. He runs away from this mother partner or, at least, refuses to let her into his inner world. Whatever his actual behavior may be, he relates, in general, to his partner more like a boy to his mother than as a man to a woman. *And the more he acts like the boy, the more she comes at him as mother.* She becomes the very thing he doesn't want.

The part of the woman that wants to grow into her fullest feminine hates having a son for a partner. Her desire is to be needed but she doesn't want to be mother to him. If he would just change, if he would grow up and be a man, she wouldn't have to be a mother. She feels like she needs to keep pressure on him, however, because she believes that if she let up on him, he might be a son forever. She has great difficulty refraining from acting out her role in the dance.

The part of the man that wants to grow into his fullest masculine hates having a controlling mother for a partner. He doesn't want the mother-son dance any more than she does. He tells himself everything would be okay if she would just be a woman and stop playing mother.

He points his finger at her accusingly, making her the problem. But he likewise has great difficulty refraining from his own role in the dance, and the pair get locked into a mother-son bonding pattern, with each partner steadfastly determined to blame the other for the problem.

We might imagine that this dynamic would become boring very quickly. Why would a man and a woman stay in such a mutually unrewarding situation? Something more must be going on in this dance, since, in real life, both parties are usually extremely reluctant to end it. In fact, if consciousness is not brought to this situation, it can go on for a lifetime.

FATHER-DAUGHTER DANCE

The father-daughter bonding pattern closely parallels the mother-son pattern. Here, however, the man adopts the parent role. Whether he demonstrates qualities of a benevolent father or a controlling father is less important than the fact that he adopts a position in the relationship as the one who "knows better."

When acting out the father role, the man uses a tone of voice of, or adopts an attitude of, superiority. He might use rational arguments to bolster his sense of being the one who is right. On the surface he may proclaim his respect for his partner as a woman, but underneath, through the eyes of his deeper psyche, he sees his partner as more of a daughter than a woman.

Men who act out the father role in their relationships often have difficulty seeing themselves clearly. The father type gets cultural support for the role he takes—that of protector and provider—and as far as he can see, he is just doing what is right. Generally speaking, he is not interested in personal growth or in understanding the hidden dynamics of his relationship. He mainly wants to hold on to his status and maintain a favorable image of himself as a powerful man.

Daughter types also get cultural support for taking their role. She serves. She supports. She mothers the children and, even if she has numerous duties outside of it, the responsibilities of the home sit mainly with her.

She is often happy with this role . . . at first. "Daughter" finds the "father" she has been looking for, and both are happy dancers. Over time, however, major problems emerge. Father types appreciate daughter types at the beginning of a relationship, but a woman who has reached middle age and still acts principally out of her daughter role tends to be boring and narrow. When the relationship gets too dull and/ or unfulfilling, the father type tends to go outside of it to seek something more.

No matter how compliant or powerless she may appear to be on the surface, the daughter partner always gets tired of being seen as a daughter by her egocentric mate. At various times in her life, she will come to the point where she must decide whether to continue catering to him in his role or attempt to balance the scales by openly challenging him for power in the relationship.

Daughter types who don't take up this challenge find themselves closing off to their partner in different ways. She, too, may find an existence outside of the relationship. She may go through the motions of intimacy but not experience full sexual enjoyment. In extreme situations, the daughter type may retreat into depression or addiction. In many cases she may just resign herself to the role and set out to make the best of it. In short, she becomes emotionally numb.

Though catering to his requirements has a numbing effect over the long run, stepping out of the daughter role is as difficult for her as stepping out of the father role is for him. Deep down she really *feels* like a daughter, and leaving her support system to move out into the world is frightening. At the same time, she knows that women who achieve some sense of power are threatening to her partner and she is terrified of the rejection she is sure would come if she were to bring forth her power.

Like the mother-son bonding pattern, the father-daughter bonding pattern gets locked into place because moving off of their spots would be difficult for both partners. To change the patterns, both partners must take on difficult tasks in the journey of expanding personal awareness— that is, in growing up.

Doug Discovers the Son and Father within Himself

We will offer much more about bonding patterns later. But now, because Naomi and I have learned that personal stories facilitate the learning of this material, I will balance the theory we've presented so far with a summary of my own personal discoveries in this area. I'll trace a few of my realizations in discovering my own emotional child and the role it has played in my relationships.

A few years ago, if anyone had told me I was an emotional child, a "son" in my relationships, I would have flatly rejected the idea. Perhaps my partner was sometimes an emotional child . . . but not me.

At age eighteen, I left home and started out into the world. I believed I had done a reasonably good job of separating from my parents and family. I began my first major relationship when I was twenty-one, and we were together for fourteen years. We were "best friends" and cared for each other very deeply. Economically, we were able to combine our energies and do well. She was steady and career- oriented. At the time, I worked in positions related to offshore oil exploration in the Arctic. It was a man's world and I felt powerful there.

On the surface, our relationship went well. However, we both had a nagging feeling that something was wrong and neither of us was able to understand what it was. Some unidentified but essential needs in both of us were not being met. Neither of us was nourished by the relation- ship as much as we expected. At times she felt these deficiencies more strongly and at times I did. We tried parting for periods of time but always came back together. At first, being back together was wonderful, yet later we felt trapped.

Our situation was similar to many I have since witnessed. Specifi- cally, we related to each other more as brother to sister than as man to woman. She seemed somehow to give me the feeling of family

64

belonging that wasn't fully available in my actual birth family. I seemed to do the same for her. I can see now that behind the facades we presented to the world (and to each other), we were a young, insecure boy and girl, trying hard to make it in a world that felt foreign. Though neither of us wanted to admit it, we were held together by our needs for security.

She found a sense of meaning and power in our relationship by taking on the mother role, just as her own mother had done with her father. As much as I wanted to see myself as a mature man, I now realize that unconsciously (through the eyes of my psyche as opposed to the eyes of my ego) I was *looking* for a mother. My habitual posture in the relationship became more like that of a "son" than that of a mature man.

With her playing the mother and my playing the son, we somehow found a measure of comfort and safety in the world. It was what we wanted but it wasn't what we *really* wanted. It didn't feed us. I resented her mothering and the way she held herself above me; she resented my son role and the way I sucked on her. I can see now that behind the friendly faces that showed on the surface of our relationship was great anger about our arrangement.

Emotionally young men are terrified of their own anger and use any number of strategies to cover it over. Furthermore, they are terrified of a woman's anger and use any number of strategies to avoid it. Instead of dealing with it, I rationalized my anger away. I played the good boy and I often avoided bringing up things that might arouse her anger. I also played the bad boy and brought her down in passive ways. My tendency was to demonstrate my anger indirectly by withdrawing— another time-honored strategy of the child.

No man plays only the son role in an intimate relationship, and sooner or later I would get tired of her being the controlling mother. The best way for me to change the situation was to adopt a father role, which, in my case, usually meant the judgmental, critical father—a character who bore an uncanny resemblance to my own father. Sure enough, as soon as I took on this role and became judgmental, she dropped from her "mother perch" and collapsed into a daughter role for a while.

For example, I would be critical of her—particularly if our sexual experience didn't live up to my ideal. I also used to criticize her body. Even if I didn't voice these judgments aloud, she seemed to sense when they were present and usually became more daughter-like in response.

When she was in the child role, she either tried harder to become perfect or seized up emotionally—withdrawing into her own world. After a short while of being the "pleaser" or being withdrawn, however, she returned to her controlling mother role. Confronted by her "mother," I fell back into a son role. Getting tired of "son," I brought out my judgmental father, which encouraged her daughter to come out for a while. She tired of playing daughter and became controlling mother— and on and on and on the dance went.

It was as though we had a repertoire of only four characters. If she wasn't the controlling mother, she was the daughter. When I wasn't playing the son, I was the judgmental father. But when it came to playing out man and woman, or any of the range *between* parent and child, we were at a loss. Occasionally we could both bring out our carefree, fun-loving child and play together, but that seemed to happen less and less as the years went by.

At the time I was largely unconscious of these inner characters. I did have a sense of her being a controlling woman. I knew that underneath *her* controlling part, she was very young and vulnerable, though she usually didn't expose it. However, I couldn't see my own role very clearly. I seldom allowed myself to become aware of how needy, powerless, and emotionally young I felt below the mask I presented to the world. I recognize now that *when a man is unconscious of being in a son role, his seeing his own responsibility in drawing out the mother role in his partner is almost impossible.* I couldn't see how controlling and judgmental I was. Like most emotional children, I tended to set

66

myself up as a victim of the circumstances around me and pointed at her as the source of our problems. Eventually we divorced.

A year or so into my second marriage, I was shocked to discover that the same dramas were unfolding again. In spite of my deliberate intentions to choose otherwise, I found myself with another controlling mother! Though Naomi appeared to be gentle and sweet at the beginning, soon enough I discovered that I had a barracuda on my hands! But I wanted her and I gradually recognized that if I was going to make our relationship work, I needed to learn how to meet her from other parts of myself than the habitual teeter-totter of father/son. In order to do that, I needed to become more honest about myself and learn to access more of my adult male.

Coming Up:

The next two chapters will feature four case histories of couples who are locked into bonding patterns. Since looking at amplified situations is often useful, chapter 6 will focus on two couples where the mother-son bonding patterns are highlighted and chapter 7 will examine the father-daughter dynamic in more detail.

Readers who are inclined to think in terms of either/or will tend to identify themselves with one bonding pattern or the other. Once again, however, we want to emphasize that relationships in real life never just go one way and are not as clearly focused as the examples we are presenting here. All men have a "father" inside and all have a "son." All women have a "mother" and a "daughter." Every relationship has both mother-son and father-daughter components, and we are simply highlighting the dynamics we wish to illustrate.

6

MOTHER-SON RELATIONSHIPS

In the previous chapter, we defined a mother-son bonding pattern as a circumstance in which the woman is playing out "mother" with a man who is acting out "son." "Mother" and "son" in this case are actually roles or *patterns of behavior* that intimate partners habitually play out with each other. The roles are so deeply ingrained that the partners are not fully conscious of what they are doing, though at least one of the partners does ultimately become dissatisfied with this way of interacting. Until they gain an awareness of what is going on underneath those roles, partners caught up in bonding patterns tend to spend their energy blaming the other for the stagnation in their relationship rather than looking inward, into their own nature, for solutions.

The following case examples show two couples with strong mother-son patterning. In selecting two couples who appear to have different issues, Naomi and I intend to demonstrate that mother and son roles can have various faces—just as real mothers and sons do. The underlying dynamic, however, is similar, and as we proceed with the analysis, we intend to show that both of these couples are facing the same challenge, the challenge of growing up and taking responsibility as adult men and

69

women. We will present both cases before the analysis, to avoid repeating points that are common between the two couples.

CASE EXAMPLE #1: Karen & Jim

Karen and Jim had been together for four years. They came to us with a number of complaints common to relationships stuck in bonding patterns. Their relationship had become passionless. They fought over a lot of small issues which both realized were relatively unimportant in the grand scheme, yet neither was willing to back down. She said she felt angry about having a partner who did not seem able to match her intensity and commitment to life. Over the previous six months they had been struggling with each other over the question of whether or not to have a baby.

Jim was thirty-eight, had a university education, and worked as a clerk in a hardware store. He gave the impression of being a gentle, considerate, soft-spoken man who seldom got angry. He liked being at home by himself and was not at ease with large groups of people. He had only a few friends, most of whom were women.

Karen, thirty-six, had worked diligently to establish a successful career as an educator. She was well-recognized in her work and brought home a good income. She appeared to be easygoing on the surface but she was also a good manager—both at work and at home. She had a wide circle of friends and thought of herself as open and accommodating.

Jim and Karen reported having enjoyed each other in the early stages of their relationship. Karen believed she had found a sensitive man who seemed capable of understanding her. She was mildly concerned about his quiet nature but was impressed by how thoughtful he was. She expected she would be able to bring him out and help him express himself more fully.

Jim believed he had finally found a partner who was willing to accept him for who he was. He liked the way she tried to please him. He noticed her tendency to want to control but liked her ambitious nature and what she was able to bring to the relationship.

According to Karen, the relationship began to deteriorate seriously when she started to think about having children. Her biological clock was ticking and she was not sure Jim would be able to support a family, financially or emotionally. Though she cared deeply for him, she had recently begun to take a more critical look and was not happy with what she saw.

She resented his lack of aggressiveness. He was passive in almost every domain. He wouldn't even take any responsibility for organizing their social events. When he was angry, instead of expressing it directly, he sniped at her with verbal barbs. He had become passive in bed and seemed to be waiting for her to define their sexuality. She found herself acting more and more like a mother, and the prospect of having to be his mother (*and* the mother of a child) was abhorrent to her.

She said Jim wouldn't share his feelings with her, though she had pleaded with him to do so. Lately he had become so withdrawn that he often didn't even seem to hear what she was saying. When he did respond, he tended to deliver an intellectual discourse. After these sermons, she usually felt confused and distanced by his words. She needed more from him.

Jim talked about how frustrated he felt. At the beginning, she seemed to accept him as he was; now she wanted to change him. These days, she appeared to be constantly complaining and criticizing him. She said she wanted him to "be a man," yet she tenaciously held on to control. A few years back he considered starting his own business but she discouraged him from taking the financial risk. He remembered a time when he did express some anger and she scolded him for days afterward, telling him how abusive he was.

Karen replied that bringing her demands into the open and expressing them directly had been difficult. Her experience was that as soon as she made any demand on him, he either defended himself by trying to out-reason her or withdrew into one of his moods. These low-grade depressions could go on for months. She was afraid of losing him, but time was passing quickly and she was not sure she wouldn't be better off without him—even if it meant risking being alone.

Part of Jim liked the idea of their having a child, but he wasn't sure he wanted to be tied down with a woman who was so critical and controlling. He never seemed able to please her. She wanted him to be powerful but seemed to want to emasculate him as well. Lately, he found himself being tempted to find relief in a bottle, but he resisted the urge, having vowed not to take the same route as his father.

CASE EXAMPLE #2: Nathan & Beverly

Nathan and Beverly had been together for fourteen years and had two children. Though they said they got along reasonably well, in their session with us, they were clearly experiencing a great deal of tension. As their story unfolded, what became clear was that both had been holding back from each other, but neither was willing to let go of the marriage.

Nathan was what might be called a "charmer," who was very successful in his career. He talked of feeling a deep bond with Beverly. He acknowledged that a lot of his sense of meaning and security came from being with her. She was the only person he really trusted with his innermost thoughts. He felt she was his "best friend."

Beverly appeared to be quite a serious person. She had been the steady one and held the family together while Nathan frequently travelled away from the home. She had given Nathan a lot of room and support because she didn't want to lose him. She, too, talked of feeling deeply bonded with him. He was a good father to her children.

Beverly was first to reveal that she felt hurt and angry about Nathan's flirtations with another woman at his workplace. He maintained that she had nothing to be concerned about. Beverly said she did not really trust him and was still feeling wounded by an affair he had several years before. She sensed that more was going on than he admitted.

Before long, Nathan brought up one of his major concerns: his sexual life with Beverly. He didn't believe he would flirt with other women if he were more fulfilled by her. Though she seldom refused him sex, he sensed she was holding back from him. She was too bland; something seemed to be missing. He talked about receiving a lot more affection from his daughters than he did from Beverly.

Beverly replied that he might get more from her if he was home more often. She was getting tired of holding down the home front alone. She wanted him to cut down on his travel and devote more time to her and the family. She didn't really trust that he was present for her.

ANALYSIS OF CASE EXAMPLES

Obviously, a lot was going on in both of these relationships but let's isolate the mother-son dynamics. Ambitious Karen wants her partner to grow up and take more responsibility so she will be able to support a baby at home. Abandoned Beverly wants her partner to grow up and stop being the play "boy." Stay-at-home Jim wants his partner to stop controlling and criticizing him so much. Charmer Nathan wants his partner to become more alive and sexually involved. In both of these relationships, some kind of standoff is clearly underway. Neither the men nor the women are getting what they want. They aren't feeling nourished and each feels as though the other is the problem.

As a way of beginning our analysis, we'll look at the relationships from the viewpoint of each of the participants. As we go along, we'll speculate more about what is underneath the surface appearances.

The Males' Viewpoints

Jim is getting tired of Karen's criticisms. He acknowledges that he withdraws but sees it as a natural response to her treatment of him. He tends to keep his thoughts to himself, since she is inclined to take everything he says and use it against him. She complains about his not being sufficiently sexually assertive, but to him it's just another sign that, in her eyes, he can do nothing right. He doesn't know how to please

73

her anymore and believes his only recourse is to hold back and wait for her to tell him what she wants. The thought of being stuck with a critical, controlling mother for the next twenty years is not appealing.

Nathan resents the limits Beverly wants to put on him. She seems always to be pressuring him to cut down on his time away from home. He is tired of her jealousy over his friendships with other women. She seems to want him to give up everything, to want complete control of his life. She says she needs a stronger commitment from him but he questions whether he really desires to deepen his commitment to someone who is not very responsive to him sexually. If he committed to her in the way she wants, he might end up less than fulfilled, with a bland woman for the rest of his days.

Nathan and Jim as Sons

Even though Jim and Nathan appear to function quite differently in their relationships, both have a strong tendency to relate to their partners from the son role. Jim acts out the good boy who is quiet, soft-spoken, and doesn't express his anger. As is typical of many son types, he tends to depend on his partner to go out into the world and be a supportive, protective mother for him.

Nathan's boy role is not as obvious as Jim's—especially insofar as he is seen outside the home. Having achieved some success in the world, he seems to have the typical trappings of a successful adult male. The charmer who loves being around woman frequently experiences social approval and is regarded as having desirable qualities of masculinity.

Nathan's son role can be seen more clearly in his home atmosphere (which partially explains why he doesn't want to be there much). At home, Nathan depends on Beverly to act out the good mother. He expects her to look after his daily physical needs and be present to support him emotionally. With Beverly playing out the good mother role, he is able to experience a relatively carefree existence. Riding his motorcycle usually has higher priority than supporting her emotional needs!

Both of these men are facing major demands from their partners. But son types, emotional boys, generally don't react favorably when demands are placed on them—especially by intimate partners. Like many real sons who don't want to feel dominated by mother, their first instinct will typically be to defend against any demands by refusing to act in the way that is demanded—even if doing so might be in their best interests. The more she tries to change him, the more defiant he will become. Were he to give in to her demands, he would feel as if something vital was being sacrificed.

The boy part of a man sees women as consuming mothers. This part feels there is no end to their voracious demands and believes the way to survive is to adopt a protective stance. In the process of developing this stance, the man learns to close off his emotions, the avenue to his vulnerability. To be closed off in this way feels, to him, like a position of strength. After all, he is protecting his soul.

The boy part has difficulty grasping that a man of age thirty-five or above who closes off emotionally under pressure from a woman is really in a type of collapse. He might silently believe he is coming from a position of strength, but it is only pseudo-strength. Unbeknownst to him, he is seen by her as weak and contracted, as hiding out. And in this case, her view is closer to the truth. From his position of defense, he is not fully able to confront or even respond to the forces coming at him from his partner, which are actually the forces coming at him from life.

There is a lot more these boy types don't know or are not willing to acknowledge about themselves and their role in the dysfunction of their relationships. So before we look at the women partners, let's go a little further and speculate about the shadow sides of these men.

THE SHADOW SIDE OF SON TYPES

Jim: What He Needs to Look at in Himself

Though he would be loath to admit it openly, Jim is a user. He expects the woman he is with to support him. He unconsciously seeks out supportive mother types as partners because, as an emotional boy, he feels powerless and needy. But he doesn't want to know about these feelings. The easiest way to continue avoiding them is to live in a fantasy world of his own mind and depend on his wife to be responsible for meeting the demands of the outer world.

Though Jim shows evidence of powerlessness on the surface, part of his shadow (as with all child partners) feels "better than." He is afraid to go out and find his own power in the world partially because of his fear of failure and partially because, secretly, he regards himself as special and superior to all that is going on around him. If he were to step out into the world and compete, as his partner is demanding he do, he would risk finding out how ordinary and powerless he really is underneath the role-mask of good boy. He prefers to stay home and be supported.

Until they become more conscious of who they are under the surface, boy types like Jim will always be attracted to women who feel their duty is to mother men. He wants a beneficent, supportive mother, but when he gets a controlling one (which, unfortunately for him, is part of the package), he doesn't like it. He prefers a "good" mother type without any strings attached. But, as Nathan has also discovered, good mothers who don't make demands are in short supply (and tend to be rather dull). As time goes by, all "mothers" will want something in return for their support, and when that demand comes, the boy-part of a man is going to be smoked out.

Jim avoids these feelings and awarenesses by staying in the world of his own mind. His mind serves as a type of sanctuary, a place where he can separate himself from the influence of those around him. But his mind is also a place where he can sustain his own delusions more easily. By keeping his thoughts and feelings to himself, he runs less risk of exposing how young he really is underneath the mask he puts on.

Nathan: What He Needs to Look at in Himself

Like all emotional children, Nathan is very self-centered and needs huge amounts of attention. Up to this point, his implicit expectation has been that Beverly will nurture and look after him, regardless of what he does outside the relationship. Just below the surface he believes his wife (i.e., "mother") should be delighted that she is being graced with his presence. (An image comes to mind of the son who thinks a great mother's day gift is to come over for dinner!)

Nathan gets an experience of power in relationship by withholding. In refusing to give Beverly what she most wants—commitment to herself and the home—boy-Nathan gets to have a sense of control over his mother partner. He keeps her on edge and feeling insecure. Of course, in the end he loses, because in that position, she will continue to withhold her full sexual participation.

Nathan exhibits another trait that is often present when an emotional child lives in an adult's body. He is a "seducer." The seducer is charming and tends to live on surface appearances. The shadow side of seducers is that they get their feelings of power and self-worth by sustaining an image that is attractive to the opposite sex. He needs to flirt because he needs women to support this self-bolstering process. However, this type of "power" is illusory, as it is totally dependent on events outside of himself. Inside, he feels small, empty, and powerless.

Even though he is not getting fulfilled sexually, Nathan is unlikely to leave his relationship with Beverly—at least not until he has found another woman (who, the chances are, will also mysteriously develop increasing amounts of mother-behavior as time goes by).

Now that we have covered some basic aspects of the men's side, we'll take a look at the women's contribution to this invisible dance.

The Females' Viewpoints

Karen wants to experience broader ranges of her feminine self, ranges that include the adult woman as well as the "mother." At this stage of her life, she senses that the way to move more deeply into her femininity is to have a child. But she needs a father for this child and, therefore, wants Jim to change, to be more of a man in ways that meet her particular requirements. He accuses her of trying to direct and control him, but she has seen before that he won't budge if she doesn't speak out (and usually not even then!). If she doesn't try to change him, she'll be stuck forever with a boy. She feels a sense of urgency and fears he will not be up to the task.

Beverly has been a good, supportive, loyal mother, providing a home base for her husband. She is tired of not being seen and appreciated for who she is and what she does. She can't understand why Nathan refuses to spend more time at home and always seems to have one eye scanning around at other women. She believes she does try to live up to his sexual expectations, though Nathan never appears to be quite happy with her. He always seems to criticize *her* sexually, but if she were to be honest, she would tell him his own sexuality seems immature and is not really very nourishing for her. She keeps this thought to herself because if she were to criticize him openly, she believes he couldn't take it.

Karen and Beverly as Mothers

Both Beverly and Karen have a tendency to relate to their partners more as mothers toward sons than as women toward men. They see themselves as the ones who are the responsible adults in the relationship. Karen sees Jim as a stubborn and withdrawn son who refuses to grow up. Beverly sees Nathan as a playful and rebellious boy who refuses to take on full responsibility for her and the family. Deep within their belief systems, both have very little trust that any man is capable of looking after them; in their minds, all men are misguided or immature and need to be mothered.

Why does a woman habitually take on the mother role with her partner when she often seems to get little in return? Why does she always find a boy type as a partner? More must be going on than meets the eye and we need to take a closer look at the situation.

The mother type gets feelings of worthiness by being needed. Being the helper or the mediator gives her a definition, an identity. By acting out a role that is virtuous and beyond reproach, she assumes she is just fine as she is. The possibility never occurs to her that her role is a defense, one as potent as the defense that is so obvious to her in her son-type partner. By adopting the mother role, she can avoid looking inward to find out who she is underneath the facade. By acting out the mother role, she gets to feel as if she is personally powerful.

In many cases the mother type had a father who was emotionally underdeveloped or otherwise distant. From her mother, she learned that all men are little boys and that the way to be with them (if at all) is to act out mother. She thus learns to define herself *by what she does for men* as opposed to defining herself by who she is inside. Taking on the mother role is the only way she knows how to relate to men she cares for. She doesn't really know how to relate as a woman because she has never seen it modeled.

In her adult years, she blames her partner for being such a boy. Yet underneath her mothering behavior, the mother type is really a needy girl of an emotional age almost exactly equivalent to that of the son she so desperately wants to see grow up. She has taken on the mother *role* so completely that she has great difficulty seeing clearly who *she*, herself, is. She focuses on her partner as the problem and thus puts her attention on trying to get *him* to change.

She points her finger at her partner for avoiding his feelings, yet denies many of her own feelings. For example, by being "mother" to those around her, she avoids her feelings of unworthiness, powerlessness, and emptiness as a woman. She sees this emotional child part being acted out by her partner and feels disgust, but the intensity of this disgust has a lot to do with her unconscious recognition of aspects of herself she has avoided most of her life. She is repelled by this little boy who refuses to grow up, yet he is actually only reflecting an inner part of *her* that exists under the mother facade she has learned to present.

As time goes by in her relationship, what the mother type does become aware of is how empty, frustrated, and unsatisfied she feels—at least in terms of her relationships with men.

THE SHADOW SIDE OF MOTHER TYPES
What Karen and Beverly Need to Look at in Themselves

One of the shadow aspects of all parent types is their instinctive inclination to choose a partner who, they believe, will not threaten their mask of power. The mother type instinctively senses that a son type will be easily controlled and not as likely to challenge her "mother cover." Not only does she get to feel worthy by rescuing a boy, but she also gets to be the one in charge. The mother type is much less likely to chose a man with authentic power, because she wouldn't know what to do with him.

In therapeutic sessions, mothers like Karen frequently talk for their partners—often making corrections or embellishments. It is their unconscious way of showing who is in charge. A mother like Beverly uses strategies that are even more indirect. She has discovered that one way to control is to be the "good mother," who quietly preserves power by making herself indispensable.

Partnering with a boy type serves the mother type in other ways. Like all parent types, Karen gets to bolster her feelings of superiority and importance by holding herself above her "immature partner." Her deeply held view that men are immature and untrustworthy is regularly validated by her partner and she can experience being a victim of them rather than looking into her own issues. Being linked with an emotional boy allows the mother type to blame her partner (and perhaps even men in general) for a life that is not as full as it should be. As much as she might feel disgusted by him, the good mother has a strong investment in the boy type not growing up.

Though their grasping this idea may be difficult at first, Beverly and Karen are both *users*. They use their partners (and, later, their children) to give themselves a feeling that life has meaning. As they play out the mother role in an attempt to look after and fix their partners, they get to have a sense of purpose. By focusing on how out of touch their partners are with feelings, they are able to avoid how out of touch they are with themselves.

Why Are Bonding Patterns So Resilient?

"Mothers" and "sons" need to recognize that they didn't come together by accident. They came together because their individual behavior patterns fit well with each other. Though mother and son appear to be very different on the surface, both have the same essential problem to work out. Unless they come to terms with that underlying issue, the pattern has a way of reinforcing itself and can play out for a lifetime. How does this happen?

Both "mother" and "son" are very young emotionally. Neither of these types has a real sense of self and both are looking outside of themselves for a definition of who they are. The son part of a man has spent most of his life avoiding his inner feelings. We have seen that a man who doesn't know his feelings doesn't really know who he is. As much as he doesn't want to admit it to himself, he lets himself be defined by his relationship. If women like him, he likes himself. If his women are happy, he is happy. If women find him attractive, he feels powerful. He acts in ways that might be inconsistent with his own needs in order to please them or avoid their anger. (To cite an extreme and interesting example, even the misogynist is a boy type who defines himself by his opposition to women.) The son type, underneath his defenses and rationalizations, feels empty and lost.

The mother part of a woman has also spent most of her life avoiding her inner feelings and doesn't know who she is underneath the role she has learned to play. She gets a sense of meaning in life from being needed and thus lets herself be defined by what she does for others. If she is needed and supportive, the mother type feels powerful. If men like her, she likes herself. She, too, acts in ways that are inconsistent with her own well-being in order to feel needed or accepted.

In the beginning of their relationship, "mother" and "son" are delighted to find one another. She gets someone to mother and he gets someone who treats him as if he is special. Her mother part feels powerful and worthwhile. Because he is liked, he likes himself and feels powerful. He likes her, which helps her like herself. Because neither has a strong sense of self, both count on the other for positive feelings about themselves.

After a while in the relationship, however, the "mothering" looks and feels controlling to the son type. He begins to feel resentful and backs away from her. She feels needy and afraid of being abandoned, but doesn't want to admit to these feelings. Instead, she comes on stronger with mother energy (the only way she really knows how to get what she wants). She can be extremely tenacious because, as a person who essentially lives vicariously through others, the mother type has a secret expectation that her partner ought be able to make it better for her.

The "son" can't look after himself properly, let alone fill the void in her life. He feels powerless and ineffectual and (not wanting to admit these feelings to himself) adopts defensive, reactive postures. He displays even more son energy. She feels more needy and abandoned and comes at him even more strongly as mother. The pattern continues.

Since her well-being depends on him, the mother type has a very strong need to "fix" her partner. He must change! She comes at him even harder. Because he doesn't know who he is, he feels limited in the ways he can respond to her attempts to change him. Through the eyes of his son part, the feminine is very formidable. As a "son," he doesn't feel he has the resources to deal with such a formidable force and retreats even deeper into his own world. The pattern continues.

Both partners are so small inside that they feel as if they need the other in order to survive. As much as they both hate it, each ultimately depends on the other for a definition of self. There is no escape and the pattern continues.

When the "mother" starts to become discouraged about the prospects of his changing (i.e., growing up), she assumes a more critical stance. When that doesn't work after many years, she numbs to him. She becomes rigid, justifying her stance by telling herself all men are hopeless boys. No matter how disgusted she may become, she is not likely to leave altogether, as she still depends on him for her definition of self.

As it becomes apparent that the "mother" is not going to change, the boy type also becomes numb. He closes off to her, becomes rigid, and retreats into his own world, silently grumbling that all women are just controllers. He is not likely to leave altogether, though, because he depends on her to care for him.

HOW CAN A COUPLE WORK
WITH MOTHER-SON BONDING PATTERNS?

Both Partners Need to Locate Themselves

The only way to interrupt bonding-pattern behavior is for both individuals to wake up to the truth of what is really happening, *when* it is happening. We have seen that one of the major difficulties in a bonding-pattern deadlock is that the partners are intently focused outside of themselves, on the other person, and thereby remain largely oblivious to what they, themselves, are feeling in the moment. In order to counter this, they must first begin to "locate themselves," to reorient their attention from other to self. At least one of the partners needs to hesitate in the midst of what amounts to automatic behavior, take a breath, and strive to become conscious of his or her own participation in the pattern. This might sound easy enough but in the heat of conflict and power struggle, pulling attention back to self can take Herculean determination and uncomfortable levels of vulnerability.

Partners will not be able to locate themselves unless they make a very deliberate effort to slow down and continually ask themselves where they are, what is going on now, and *what they are feeling*. When a mother-son bonding pattern is dominant in a relationship, the woman needs to become alert to the experience of controlling, scolding, and criticizing. She needs continually to be asking herself whether she feels like a woman at any given moment with her partner or whether she feels like a mother relating to a son.

The man needs to become alert to the experience of withdrawing, rebelling, and withholding. He needs continually to be asking himself whether he feels like a man at any given moment with his partner or like

83

a boy. If he is feeling like a boy, he must be willing to bring this feeling into the open rather than hiding from it and pretending he is someone other than who he is at that moment. Presenting a macho facade only reinforces bonding patterns.

Work at Catching It the Moment It's Happening

Bonding-pattern behavior is triggered with lightning rapidity; its pull resembles that of an instinct. And once bonded partners are busy playing their roles, changing the course of things becomes increasingly difficult. They become more invested in unconsciously acting out the roles than in being awake to themselves.

It helps a great deal if one can train oneself to become alert to cues that bonding-pattern behavior is incipient. I used to become alert when Naomi was moving into her mother role by the way the pitch of her voice went up. She also had a certain look in her eyes. As she got better at controlling it, I could see her brooding for a while before she unleashed "mother." When this happened, I had an instinctual tendency to retreat into my own thoughts or find some other way to protect or defend myself. If I could become aware of her behavior or of my tendencies at the moment they were happening and put words to what was going on, we could head off another round of bonding-pattern behavior.

Similarly, Naomi could see when I was moving into the son role by the way I avoided eye contact. In more advanced situations I would totally withdraw into myself. Essentially I was asleep—perhaps telling myself stories about how wronged or misunderstood I was. Perhaps I was thinking about what I'd do when I got out of this relationship!

If she could catch me going into "son" or herself acting out some unsolicited "mother" behavior then put words out that I was able to hear, the bonding pattern behavior could be interrupted. Catching bonding patterns at the moment they are happening was not easy, but once we located ourselves and became alert to incipient bonding-pattern behavior, changing our course became relatively easy. As we experienced the very large difference between unconscious bonding-pattern behavior and juicy relating, the inspiration to stay alert was heightened day by day.

Adopt an Attitude of Discovery

We have seen that partners caught in bonding patterns are equally oblivious to what is truly going on. In most cases a man in relationship is not conscious that he usually is acting out a son role when he withdraws emotionally from his mate. He is generally not conscious that he is as controlling as he perceives his partner to be. He is just being the only way he knows how to be—probably a way he learned from his own father. Emotional self-control is expected of men in our culture and they are caught by the myth of the strong, silent type. When he is withdrawn into himself, he may believe he is experiencing masculine power but from the viewpoint of his partner he is simply boxed in, defended from his feelings, and without any real power to act.

At the same time, the woman is not conscious that she is acting out of a mother role; she is just doing what seems natural to her. Mothering is expected of females in our culture, and as she takes on the mother role, she seems to be experiencing a type of feminine power. She has difficulty grasping that the beloved role of "mother" is a part of her defense and keeps her as disconnected from her own feelings as her partner is from his. The mother type may think she is in her adult feminine but, as she is viewed by her partner, she is barely present as a flesh-and-blood, feeling woman.

Both partners must wake up to their mutual lack of knowing and resolve to discover more about what is going on underneath the mother-son trap they are in. Once again, this is not an easy task. Both partners need to be willing to question themselves and the deeply ingrained, habitual, outdated roles they have adopted. Both need to go inside and look at themselves in ways that are not enhancing to their self-images. The task is made all the more difficult by the fact that the immature child within will *always* resist this type of work—preferring to believe an easier solution must exist!

Keep Communicating

Keeping the lines of communication open is very important if a couple is to avoid getting stuck in bonding patterns. Both individuals need to be consistently advising each other about what is going on internally for them and cuing the other to wake up when the other falls back into habitual behavior patterns. Personal statements that expose oneself usually prove to be much more constructive than "talking about" an issue or pointing out the other's role.

Telling Naomi I didn't want her to be mother didn't usually help too much; she usually came up with some defensive, self-justifying reply ("It's your fault and I need to be this way because you are acting like a child"). However, if I responded by saying how I was *feeling*—i.e., "scolded" or "judged"—she was more inclined to stop and look at herself. If she did that, the spell of the pattern was broken and we could proceed to discover more about what was really going on underneath the surface in each of us at the moment.

Similarly, if she came to me with how she felt "abandoned" or "small" or "unappreciated," I responded more quickly and directly than when she said, "You're sulking again!"

Be Determined

Becoming aware of and learning to alter bonding-pattern behavior is a formidable task and let's not pretend otherwise. Striving to become more aware takes a great deal of determination. We have already seen that bonding patterns run deep and have a strong tendency to reappear automatically whenever consciousness is lost. Waking up is not a one-time process; it's more like lifetime work.

In the early stages of this personal growth, a test can reappear every few minutes! I estimate that Naomi and I spent about three years struggling to become aware of the occasions when we were caught in a bonding pattern. When the pattern overwhelmed us, we could get stuck for prolonged periods of time—and we still do get caught from time to time when we forget to remember.

Bring Some Humor into the Situation

This business of becoming aware doesn't have to be so serious, and mixing in a little humor can help a lot. For example, whenever I caught Naomi shifting to her mother role, instead of reverting to one of my boy-strategies, I might address her by her mother's name and say something like, "Thanks for the advice, Millie." That would get her attention! Or, when she caught me withdrawing as my father did, her imitating his mannerisms helped wake me up.

Another way to have fun with bonding patterns (and learn a lot) is to exaggerate them. I would call Naomi "Ma" and she would call me "Sonny" while we played out the roles to the extreme. We also played them out the other way when a father-daughter bonding pattern was up.

Deal More Constructively with Anger

Couples who have been caught in bonding patterns invariably experience a great deal of anger toward each other (even though it may be hidden). The immature child within each of them is afraid of anger and is reluctant to express it openly. A boy type must learn how to express his anger to his partner authentically, directly, and constructively. Similarly, a controlling mother must learn to bring her anger forward in ways other than through complaining and finding fault. This is a big task which can also be greatly facilitated by some good therapeutic help. We'll be examining this topic more thoroughly in chapter 11.

Coming Up:

Every relationship has a father-daughter component as well. Though surface appearances may be different, we will discover that the underlying elements are almost exactly the same as the mother-son bonding pattern.

7

FATHER-DAUGHTER RELATIONSHIPS

A father-daughter relationship is one in which the man habitually acts out the role of father and the woman plays out the role of daughter. Neither is conscious of playing the roles; they are both just acting in the way they have learned to behave with the opposite sex and doing what they believe is expected of them. Father-daughter bonding patterns fit more closely with stereotyped cultural expectations of male-female behavior, but they hold the same kinds of difficulties as mother-son relationships.

In this chapter, Naomi and I will present two examples of couples who demonstrate a pronounced father-daughter patterning. Once again we've picked couples who appear on the surface to have different issues but underneath are struggling with the same basic problems.

CASE EXAMPLE #1: Bob & Helen
Bob was a physician and Helen a homemaker. Married twelve years, they had two children. When they came into our office, the anger was almost palpable. Helen's initial complaint was that Bob didn't spend enough time at home with her and the children. When he was at home,

he didn't do much to help her. Later in the session, she said she couldn't stand the way he objectified and rationalized everything.

Bob was resentful because he was working hard to make money, which Helen seemed to have few qualms about spending. Nothing he did seemed to please her for any length of time. His principal gripe had to do with the sexual distance Helen maintained from him. She always seemed to be too tired.

At age thirty-five, Bob was accomplished in his profession. Though warm in his presentation of himself, he was not what one would have described as a feeling person. He articulated his views with astute, concise, rational arguments. When the topic of feelings came up, he openly acknowledged that he didn't allow feelings to get in the way of his rational assessments.

Helen appeared to be very friendly (perhaps to everyone except Bob). She was his same age and what might be described as a "helper," with a very strong desire to do things perfectly. She paid much attention to her appearance and had learned how to keep herself attractive. A feeling type, she was less afraid than Bob to show her vulnerability.

Both acknowledged that earlier in their relationship, they were happy with each other. He enjoyed having an attractive, sensitive woman around him whose major aim was to please. She was excited having a talented man with a promising career; it was the fulfillment of her dream.

But in the second decade of their marriage, things were not so rosy. Helen had enrolled in a course to further her education and felt frustrated about not having time to achieve the high standards she would like to have maintained. Bob didn't try to stop her, but he didn't try to help her in any way, either. She said it was almost as if he wanted to sabotage her efforts to develop a life outside the home.

Bob then talked about how tired he was when he came home. He didn't feel appreciated for all he provided. He did not regard helping her with the housework as the best use of his time. If she wanted to get out of the house, money was available to pay for help. He didn't believe he was holding her back and resented being blamed by her. Later in the session, he talked about being sexually starved. They had developed a way to deal with sexuality whereby he had to get her verbal consent before he could initiate sex with her, and evidently she didn't give it all that often.

Helen talked about how tired she was from all of her responsibilities. If he would carry more of the load, she wouldn't be as tired and would be more open to sex. She resented Bob's assumption that his work was more important than hers. Bob countered that he resented her taking on an even greater load by going to school. And why should he want to be home more when she had become so bitchy, critical, and sexually rejecting?

CASE EXAMPLE #2: Julia & Donald

Julia and Donald had been living together for two years. Julia was a successful businesswoman with two young teenage boys from her previous marriage. Donald was a wealthy businessman who travelled extensively. He had two daughters who lived with his ex-wife. Julia recently brought the relationship to a crisis and Donald agreed to come for counseling in an attempt to salvage it.

They had started off together in a fairy-tale existence. Donald adored Julia and showered her with attention. He was generous and lavished presents on her. He kept track of where she was at all times and arranged his activities so he could be with her as much as possible. He was interested in her appearance and frequently went shopping with her for clothes and jewelry. He suggested that she was like a "diamond in the rough," and with a little polishing (from him), her fullest being would really shine through. He encouraged Julia to sell her business so she could have more time with him. He assured her that she would never have to worry about security again.

Julia was cautious at first, then after a while began to depend on him more and more. After her first marriage broke down, she pursued a career with determination, but now she could relax. She felt good about having someone who really seemed to care for her well-being. She didn't need any of his gifts, but enjoyed the way he gave her attention. A part of her wanted to live up to the "diamond" image he saw in her.

About a month prior to their visit with us, Donald's father died. Donald received an ultimatum from his ex-wife and two daughters that, if he brought Julia to the funeral, they wouldn't attend. Donald told Julia it would be best if she didn't accompany him. Under the circumstances, Julia wanted to be understanding but, after a few days of mulling it over, couldn't hide her feelings of disappointment and anger. For the first time in their two years together, she challenged his decision. She recalled that his eyes became very steely and he told her she had no choice in the matter.

In the weeks following the funeral she began to look at their relationship more closely. She noticed that he frequently interrupted their conversations in mid-sentence to make business calls. He was so invested in her appearance and behavior that she began to feel as though she was an object rather than a person. She started to become more aware of his power over her and how afraid she was to come forward with her true feelings.

One evening, another situation arose in which she challenged his control by bringing out her feelings. She told him she felt she was really just an "armpiece." His steely controller came out momentarily and made it clear that she was overstepping the boundary he held to be appropriate. Then, essentially ignoring what she had said, he began telling her how beautiful she was and insisted on proclaiming how perfect their relationship was—just the way it was. After that episode, she threatened to leave him.

ANALYSIS OF CASE EXAMPLES

In both of these relationships, the men have lived up to the masculine cultural ideal by achieving success and recognition in the world. Yet in their personal relationships, they find themselves with women who are clearly not satisfied with them and, in one case, even threatening to end the relationship.

The women in these two relationships look a little different on the surface but their essential complaint is the same. Both feel they are not being recognized and respected in some essential way. Both feel they are being submerged or suffocated in the relationship and a (growing) part of them wants to break away from it. Each feels as if she will not be able to know herself as a separate individual if she carries on without major changes in the relationship.

In a way similar to the mother-son pattern we explored in the last chapter, both of these couples are in a type of stand-off. Not any of the partners are getting enough of what they want, nor do they feel very nourished.

We'll begin an analysis of these relationships starting on the surface, then proceeding inward toward some of the underlying issues. First, each person's viewpoint.

THE FATHERS

Bob's Viewpoint

As a physician, Bob has been trained to take charge and direct others. He works long hours, and changing gears when he comes home is difficult for him. For him to justify doing housework and helping with the kids is also difficult. He feels that Helen should appreciate his hard work and the money he brings home. Instead, she seems to want to undermine him.

She accuses him of not having any feelings. He doesn't even really know what feelings are—except perhaps that they can be dangerous in the work he does. He values the capacity to use words with precision and wishes she would grow up and look at things more rationally. The points he makes have rational validity, so why can't she just accept them?

His relationship with Helen has many good aspects, but he is getting tired of being rejected sexually. Over the years she has become less and less interested in sex, giving him all manner of reasons to avoid intimate contact. Now that he has to ask her permission to initiate sex, he finds it demeaning. Silently, he's beginning to wonder if his marriage is going to make it.

Donald's Viewpoint

Donald feels baffled by what is going on with Julia. He is strongly attracted to her and, as far as he is concerned, has done "all the right things" and given her everything she wanted. He couldn't understand why she was reluctant to give up her work and accept his support. If she would only follow his guidance and accept all he had to offer, everything would be okay. After all, they seem to have a great time together.

He can't understand why she made such a fuss about not going to his father's funeral. He can't figure out why she is so sensitive. Perhaps if he humors her by going to therapy, she'll get over it.

Bob and Donald as Fathers

Looking at these case examples, we know that bonding patterns are present, because Bob and Donald tend to relate to their partners more as fathers toward daughters than as men toward women. They see themselves as being the ones who are responsible, the "adults" in the relationship. Bob regards himself as the provider and can't understand why Helen isn't content staying at home to care for him and the family. Donald believes that if Julia would only accept his support and guidance, everything would be fine.

Both men are experiencing a dilemma common to father types. The way they see it, they are trying hard to please their partners. They do, they accomplish, they support. These men believe they are playing out their roles as they are supposed to, yet they're being rejected by their partners. They cannot figure out what is going wrong and they have considerable difficulty seeing that they have any part in the problem.

The father type defines himself by what he does outwardly, but underneath his mask, he doesn't really know who he is. He doesn't want to be challenged and thus unconsciously seeks vulnerable daughter types who try hard to please their fathers. If the daughter type is content to stay in her role, the match can last a lifetime. He holds on to his image and the daughter gets the father she needs. Unfortunately, the reality of things is seldom so simple.

Even the most persevering daughter type will usually have some urges to move out of her daughter role into a fuller, more adult feminine. She wants to know her power. If she is in relationship with a father type, part of this process will involve unseating her father partner from his position of power over her. The usual way of starting this process is to reject him in some way.

Donald's partner is rejecting him outright by threatening to end the relationship. Bob's partner is rejecting him in a more subtle but no less effective way, since a time-honored strategy for making a partner small is to reject him (or her) sexually. A good daughter type might continue going through the motions, but she makes it clear in subtle ways that she is not fully present for him in bed. The father type, who wants more than anything to see himself as potent, finds himself slighted in the bedroom.

Clearly, something is going on in these relationships other than what is obvious to the persons involved. In fact, powerful, *unrecognized* feelings are strongly affecting all of them, feelings they would ordinarily be loath to become aware of or disclose. In order to get a better understanding, then, let's explore the shadow side of father types.

THE SHADOW SIDE OF FATHER TYPES

The father part of a man sees women as girls in need of his support. A man who sees women as emotional children is holding himself in a "better than" position. Though he may protest loudly how much he values women and supports their having power, a father type chooses a daughter type to marry because he wants to be with someone who will not, he believes, threaten his role.

Father types want to give support to their "daughters" but are usually not as clear about what they expect in return. They want their "daughters" to be perfect. They want the daughters to be attractive in order to reflect well on them. A father type also expects his partner to comply with his wishes and be supportive of his endeavors to achieve even more power.

Father types (like the mother types we explored in the previous chapter) often have great difficulty connecting with their deeper feelings. They *believe* their own mask and, in the eyes of their ego, are more mature than those around them. They have learned to puff themselves up in the world and refuse to acknowledge the vulnerability they experience behind their masks. They frequently have little awareness of how defended and controlling they are underneath their facades.

Bob: What He Needs to Look at in Himself.

Bob is not being completely honest. He would much rather maintain the status quo, with Helen staying at home and carrying on as before. He would get to continue the father role and thus avoid having his dominant position threatened. On some level, his partner is already aware of this and would feel less confused if it were out in the open.

He needs to see that while his show of competence serves him well in his duties as a physician, at home he must become more vulnerable. All his life he has tried to avoid feelings of inadequacy by trying hard to do things perfectly. But since mutually sustaining intimacy depends on having feelings available, no matter how difficult they may be to accept, he needs to bring forth more aspects of himself and recognize how he holds back.

Bob needs to understand that the father part of him actually *needs* his partner to be powerless and less than fully sexually mature. If he were to be with a woman who was in her power, the part of him that feels inadequate and powerless would risk being exposed and perhaps even overwhelmed.

Donald: What He Needs to Look at in Himself.

Donald's lessons are very similar to Bob's. It's a fairly easy bet that Donald has acted out a father role most of his life—going right back to his relationship with his mother early on. Playing the "father" might have provided him with a useful identity and helped him to function in the world, but it won't work in intimate relationship, where a flesh-and-blood man with ordinary feelings is called for. Just as we saw with the mother type in the previous chapter, his role serves as a way for him to avoid his inner self.

Usually Donald plays the role of the good, beneficent father but when Julia doesn't play out her role as *she* should—when she challenges him—she starts to get hints of the emergence of the bad father, the steely tyrant, who makes it clear through nonverbal expression that she had better toe the line.

Until he comes to a better understanding of his need for power and begins to recognize that he needs a lot of power to counterbalance the degree of powerlessness he feels below the surface, we can predict that Donald's intimate life will be limited. Eventually, the chances are that if Julia does leave, he will seek another daughter type who refuses to grow up and take on her own power. If this new partner refuses to challenge him, Donald is not likely to expand much beyond the point he has reached in his present relationship.

THE DAUGHTERS

Though Helen and Julia don't seem to be similar on the surface, we can sense how they both relate to their partners from their daughter parts. Both are looking for an attentive, powerful father—probably the one they never really emotionally experienced in their childhood.

Helen's Viewpoint

At first Helen was drawn to Bob's brilliance. She liked the fact that he was driven, ambitious, and self-assured. He seemed to excel in everything he did. Now, however, she feels overshadowed by him. She doesn't feel she can really talk with him, because he has a way of using words to turn everything back on her. Whenever she tries to share her feelings, he quickly responds by suggesting some type of strategy she ought to use to solve her "problem."

Over the years she has begun to notice how he uses his rational capacities to defend himself and to make others, herself in particular, look smaller. Not only can he be extremely critical, but he also is closed emotionally most of the time. Try as she does, she is not able to feel as fast as he thinks. She gets drawn into rational arguments and usually ends up feeling defeated. At the same time, she feels starved emotionally when he won't share his feelings with her.

It seems to her as if the only time he touches her is when he wants sex. She didn't say anything about that for a long time but couldn't get over feeling she was being used by him. She wants him to touch her just for the sake of touching her—at least some of the time. She doesn't want to cut him off altogether sexually, but she has reached the point where she "freezes" every time he comes close to her, because she anticipates being used again. The only way she could imagine making things easier for herself was to ask him to declare ahead of time when he wanted sex, so she could prepare herself and counter her tendency to contract. She was sure she would get over this reaction if he simply learned to touch and hold her, without demanding anything more.

She cares for Bob and doesn't want to break up the family. She likes the security and financial stability he provides. Increasingly, however, she has been feeling smothered and used. He isn't supportive of her going out and finding herself. Lately she has been thinking she might be better off without him. It's as though things are just "good enough" to stay in the marriage but, she wonders, is "good enough" enough?

Julia's Viewpoint

When Donald whispered in her ear that she would never need to worry because he would look after everything, it was like a siren's song to Julia. Above all else, she wanted to hear that from a man, yet now she feels she sold herself out in some way. As long as she was compliant and allowed Donald to make her over in the image he was seeking, things went along fine. He gave to her as long as he was getting everything his way. As soon as she challenged him, she discovered there was a cost.

She realized that in order to placate him, she had been burying her feelings, playing the role of good girl. She wanted to be the "diamond" and was trying hard to be perfect, to live up to the image he held of her. She also realizes now that she is afraid of him.

She still cares for Donald and she'd like to have the relationship be the way it was in the beginning. Right now, however, she strongly doubts she can be true to herself and be in the relationship, too.

THE SHADOW SIDE OF DAUGHTER TYPES
Helen: What She Needs to Look at in Herself

No less than father types, daughter types want it all—their way. Helen expects Bob to provide amply for her, to relieve her of her workload, and to support her in her endeavors outside the house. She wants him to let go of the way he controls her through his rationality. In short, she doesn't really want him as a man; she wants an ideal father for a partner, a father who will adore her and give her everything she wants.

She talks about being controlled by Bob, but sexually *she* is very controlling. She has figured out a way to keep him guessing and believing he can never quite do it right. She finds a sense of power she doesn't experience in the other realms of her life by denying Bob the thing he most wants: her sexual openness.

Helen complains about the way Bob sabotages her attempts to go out into the world and establish herself. But there are parts of herself she doesn't want to see. She is inflated and has a huge fear of failure; if she can't do something perfectly and with wide acclaim, she doesn't want to do it at all. Underneath everything, she is lazy and doesn't really want to put in the time that is required to excel. She also feels *special*, and the work she could get in the early stages of a career would not give her an income that would support these feelings of specialness. Thus, daughters like Helen get to live vicariously through the accomplishments of their partners without having to reveal their sense of inadequacy.

Julia: What She Needs to Look at in Herself

The shadow side of the "pleaser" figures out what people want and behaves accordingly to get attention and affection. It's not a steely type of control but it's a powerful manipulation nonetheless. Julia now is able to see how her partner controls and manipulates her, but has difficulty seeing how controlling she, herself, is. She can see how egocentric and self-involved her partner is, but now must look inward to see that the same goings-on are a major part of her story, too!

People who spend their lives trying to live up to the image of another will experience huge amounts of anger, whether they show it or not. They are being used. Julia was experiencing anger right from the beginning and has been unwilling to acknowledge it within herself. She doesn't really know who she is or what she feels. Most of her attention has been oriented toward her outer image.

Finding her anger took two years. Many daughter types require a lot longer than that because they have difficulty taking responsibility for expressing their anger directly. Now, rather than finding out more about her anger and risking expressing it, Julia prefers to cut and run.

Child types set themselves up in their own minds as victims of their overpowering partners. In Julia's case, pointing her finger at him for not *allowing* her to express her feelings is much easier than taking responsibility for her own experience. Rather than looking into how she is responsible for the situation she is in and finding a way to bring up her power to meet his, she opts for sudden abandonment, rendering Donald powerless by use of a passive strategy.

HOW CAN A COUPLE WORK
WITH FATHER-DAUGHTER BONDING PATTERNS?

In these last two chapters we have been treating father-daughter bonding patterns in relationship as if they were a phenomenon distinct from mother-son bonding patterns. As we shall see more clearly in the next chapter that was only an arbitrary distinction in order to simplify our exposition. Any relationship that has father-daughter bonding-pattern behavior also has mother-son behavior (and vice versa). And both patterns are equally detrimental to passionate, fulfilling relationship.

The prescription we gave for working with mother-son bonding-pattern behavior at the end of the last chapter is no different from the one we suggest for working with father-daughter bonding-pattern behavior. Partners who see themselves acting out a father-daughter pattern need first to *locate* themselves, stop putting so much critical attention on the other, and become more conscious of their own individual contributions to the pattern. It takes two to act out their roles and to keep behavior patterns in place.

Part of the truth that father and daughter types need to face together is that until they become more aware of themselves, theirs is often more a "using" relationship than a love relationship. Father types use their partners to help bolster an image of power. As they keep themselves busy "doing" things for their helpless partners, father types also get to avoid looking at who they are inside. Daughter types use their partners to avoid going out into the world and finding out who they really are. They get security. They get to sit back and see themselves as victims of male power.

If the daughter type is going to become a more mature woman, she must come out from behind her emotional child mask and discover who she is. By feeling her feelings and learning how to express them outwardly, she can come to terms with her fear of men and her anger toward them. Learning about her anger and then being willing to express it directly is of utmost importance for a daughter type. Realistically speaking, her partner is not likely to make the first move.

For his relationship to move beyond the image level into deeper levels of intimacy, the father type must also be willing to tap into his true feelings, the feelings below his power-image. This often proves to be difficult because the image of power becomes encrusted as the years go by. As the father type becomes more respected and even honored for his achievements in the outer world, he will probably be less willing to acknowledge that he might be retarded in terms of his emotional nature and capacity for intimacy. He is not likely to seek therapeutic help on his own, because part of his image is built on telling himself he knows more than those around him.

Rather than going into his own feelings, the extreme father type has a strong tendency to focus on his partner as the problem. She becomes the "patient," and a true daughter type often willingly takes on the role. For example, Naomi and I have seen several instances where the father type becomes very involved in his partner's decision to have a breast implant—with the expectation that surgery would help salvage the relationship. As a result of the operation, she would feel more worthwhile and by her thus having been "fixed," things would improve for both of them.

Rather than fixing his partner, he needs to recognize that she is showing him something within himself that he needs to reclaim. Powerful as he may be on the outside, inside and hidden he has all the feelings of unworthiness and vulnerability he can so easily see in her. As he becomes more self-aware, he needs to examine his fear of feminine power and his drive to be in control by taking care of women.

Locating themselves is the first step, because partners need to arrive where they are before there is any real hope of moving anyplace else. Once the partners in a father-daughter bonding pattern have begun to locate themselves, we suggest they follow up with the same prescriptions we listed in the last chapter for dealing with mother-son bonding patterns. They need to use their will and determination to work at catching their bonding-pattern behaviors at the moment they are happening. Honest communication needs to come forth—with particular emphasis on whatever they are feeling at any given moment. A good sense of humor will help a great deal.

A willingness by both father and daughter types to adopt an attitude of discovery is of utmost importance because, like the mother and son types, the father and daughter types hold the keys for each other's progress toward well-being.

Coming Up:

In the next chapter we will put the mother-son dance and father-daughter dance together, to see how bonding patterns operate in relationship.

PART FOUR

Control, Children, Sex, and Anger

8

I'D RATHER BE IN CONTROL
THAN BE HAPPY

Switching to a discussion of control issues might seem like a radical departure from the mother-son and father-daughter dynamics of the previous chapters. Actually, however, it is not. The struggle for control and power in an intimate relationship is closely interrelated with these parent-child bonding patterns. In this chapter we'll attempt to get closer to the roots of this frustrating phenomenon.

We have seen that when couples are caught in bonding patterns, neither partner feels completely happy and nourished. Essential needs are not being met. Partners have contracted emotionally and, though everything might function reasonably well on the surface, the point can come at which partners are so withdrawn into their own camps that they hardly even make eye-to-eye contact. Neither one can understand why things are happening the way they are and both feel powerless to change their patterns of behavior. In terms of intimate relating, they are essentially at a standstill with each other.

A silent struggle is going on. But a struggle means there must be two combatants. How can this be? How can bonded couples get themselves into such mutually unfulfilling deadlocks when the child partner doesn't appear to have sufficient power to match the parent partner? One would expect the parent partner to have control, with the child partner in a subordinate position.

In real life, however, it doesn't work out that way. In a bonding-pattern deadlock, both partners are equally capable of thwarting and frustrating the other! Both suffer in equal proportion, which suggests that both must have approximately equivalent amounts of power and both must be contributing equally to the problem.

In order to gain more understanding about this situation, Naomi and I asked clients who were acting out the child role about their perception of who had most of the control in the relationship. They always pointed to the partner who was acting out the parent role. Then, when parent partners were willing to be more vulnerable than usual, we asked them who they perceived as having the real power in the relationship. Interestingly, we discovered that they usually pointed to the child partner. So what was really going on?

Neither the parent partner nor child partner really has much self-awareness; both are mainly playing habitual roles. When neither partner has an authentic sense of self, both are focusing their attention on the other. With so much of their attention focused out on the other, each adopts the belief that the other is responsible for what is going on. Attributing responsibility to the other also means that they attribute control to the other. When both feel the other has all the control, both will experience the need to strive very hard to get some of it back. When both are fighting so hard for a sense of control, power struggles inevitably run rampant all through the relationship.

Having accumulated a great deal of personal experience in this area, we have a lot to say about it. So let's begin this segment of our exploration by dissecting the underlying struggle for control in bonded relationships. Then we'll trace backward and speculate briefly about the family upbringing that spawns individuals who find themselves deadlocked in bonding patterns. Finally, we'll close this chapter by looking at the challenges for couples who are caught in bonding patterns and the consequences of their not bringing these dynamics and feelings to conscious awareness.

THE DANCE OF CONTROL

In a bonded relationship, as we have seen, one partner gets an experience of potency and efficacy by playing out the parent role. We also have seen that the partner who is playing out the child role refuses to accept an inferior position relative to the partner. Child partners may appear to be weaker or more passive on the surface, but underneath, they are in a fierce struggle for control and are eminently capable of rendering their partner powerless. Their movements are just more subtle. In order to become clearer about this, we need to look at some of the ways that child partners typically get power in a relationship.

The Child Partner Uses Passive Strategies for Control

Like most human beings, partners who habitually play out the child role (son or daughter types) will, relative to their parent partner, stay in a powerless position only so long (sometimes mere seconds!) before getting tired of feeling that way and initiating some strategy to regain a sense of control. "Initiating," however, is not quite the right word here because it suggests that a deliberate process has taken place, whereas most of this occurs on an unconscious level. Actually, what they do is to "behave," or perhaps we should say "react," in ways that give them the sense of having power.

Child partners tend to feel blocked in regard to directly bringing forth their power. And when they are feeling powerless relative to their parent partner (which is almost all the time), they usually resort to *indirect*, childlike strategies to balance the power. An analogy comes to mind of the terrorist facing an opponent who is perceived as having vastly superior strength. A direct confrontation (meaning, in terms of the child partner, an expression of anger and outrage) would risk annihilation, so the terrorist needs to seek out the most vulnerable areas in the opponent and strike when the opponent's guard is down. Thus, the terrorist will figure out what the opponents need most in order to function successfully and find ways of denying them that. And dedicated terrorists are willing to sacrifice their own needs (perhaps even their own lives) in order to defeat the opponent. When the facades are removed, the child partner feels much the same way.

Son-Mother

Men acting out the child role often withdraw emotionally when they want to punish their partner for being too powerful. This passive strategy of withdrawing is potent because women, in general, need to hear words and receive feelings in order to feel fully nourished. The woman from whom a man has withdrawn feels as if he has cut off one of her lifelines.

When he withdraws, she is thwarted from getting what is essential to her. Since she is denied what is essential, she begins to feel needy (which means: less powerful). A woman who has adopted the mother role as her mask has great difficulty openly acknowledging neediness (such would require too much vulnerability), so rather than experiencing her neediness and expressing her feelings directly, she opts for the indirect route of trying to get him to change. If she could only get him, on his own, to deliver what she needs, her problem would be solved.

So she calls out even louder for feelings from him. He, however, is still in his child-boy and, whenever he hears anything that sounds like a demand from "mother," he withdraws even further. In his own mind, this is a show of strength on his part, because he will not be controlled by her! She then gets even less of what she needs and calls out even louder. He withdraws even more and on it goes, an insidious and destructive, self-perpetuating circle.

The mother type is accepting at first, since all parent types expect to give much more than they get back. But as time goes by, she begins to feel increasingly hungry without really understanding why. She can't quite articulate it but she somehow feels she is being punished for not doing things right (which means: his way). Anger begins to push up inside of her. Being a mother type, she is very uncomfortable with anger and her main tendency is to repress it—sometimes so deeply she doesn't even know she is feeling it. Perhaps she gets a headache instead.

Probably nothing will happen to change the pattern they are in, so it is likely to get even worse. The anger builds.

As the anger accumulates and is not released, she begins to close sexually. He then senses himself being punished by her closing sexually. He feels anger but, being in his child part, refuses to express it. Instead, he withdraws even more (perhaps protecting himself with words). He gets indigestion and/or watches more sports. Before long, a deadlock has been created, with two very angry partners blaming one another for what's going on.

Now let's take a look at what happens on the father-daughter side of things.

Daughter-Father

A woman acting out the child role in a relationship eventually gets tired of feeling powerless. She, too, uses the strategy of withdrawing as a way of punishing her partner for holding himself above her. She might turn away from him and become totally absorbed in the children or in activities outside the relationship. Along with that, she frequently withdraws sexually.

Sometimes her sexual withdrawal is deliberate (a conscious choice), but more often she just finds herself not being fully stimulated and responsive to her partner. A really good daughter type might even blame herself for being dysfunctional, rather than delving into her real feelings about her partner. Another daughter type might go through the motions of sexual intimacy but get the message across that she is doing her duty more than participating joyfully.

Her strategy of withdrawing is very potent because, as we noted earlier, men who want to act out the parent role are especially vulnerable with regard to their sexual potency. The more she withdraws, the more he is left not only undernourished but disempowered as well. As time goes by, he feels increasingly needy and eventually angry *but* he has cut himself off from access to his deeper feelings. He doesn't know where to go from this point except perhaps to try harder in the outer world, where he does seem to get respect and rewards.

The father-daughter pair goes through a dance that is similar to the mother-son drama. She feels powerless relative to him and withdraws. Like the mother type, the father type starts to feel "hungry." He expresses his hunger in terms of needing more from her sexually (not necessary more actual sexual intercourse but more of her sexual presence). Being in her child role, she senses a demand and shuts him out even more. He gets angrier but is unwilling to show it, in part because he is afraid of anger, and in part because he would have to expose his neediness (which, as we have seen, is one of the last things the parent type wants to do).

Rather than feel his need and powerlessness in this situation, the father type tries even harder to regain feelings of power. A good way for him to do this is to identify his partner as the troubled "patient," with himself the helping "father." On the surface she might allow herself to become the patient, but in her soul, she won't be dominated and withdraws even more. Eventually he goes farther outside the home to find fulfillment. She gets less and gives less, and on it goes as the distance increases between them. Both are finally just as deadlocked as their mother-son counterparts.

If all of this sounds a little bleak, hold on. We're not finished yet! The child partners don't always go for power using hidden terrorist strategies. As part of the dance of control, they often utilize more active strategies to gain power in the relationship.

The Child Becomes a Parent

The partner who habitually acts out the child role can achieve power and control in the relationship in another way: by adopting the parent role! After child types have some life experience with their partners, they "know" their parent partners are really just child types under their facades. If the right buttons are pushed, the parent type will revert to child behavior. In an intimate relationship, learning which buttons to press doesn't take long!

This might seem a little confusing until we remember the shadow side of the child type. Deep down, underneath that cherubic or sometimes sullen, defiant face, child types often do not feel as powerless as they appear to be on the surface. They are just playing a trick on the world—pretending not to have power!

Pretending not to have power is generally an ineffective way to achieve success in the outer world but here it has its advantages. By staying inside a shell, child types get to feel safe. Also, since child types abhor failure, by their playing this role, they don't risk failure—because they don't have to do anything! By keeping up a facade of powerlessness, they don't have to risk being smoked out of their secret delusions of power and specialness. They can sit back and point their fingers at others, blaming them for the world's problems.

When child types are in an intimate relationship and the hidden parts emerge, they go for control with as much (and perhaps even more) ferocity as any parent type. And because their strategies are less visible to the untrained eye, they can exercise control in an even more potent way, as what they're doing is unrecognized and generally unsuspected.

With this understanding, we can now examine how this actually works in a relationship.

The Son Type Becomes a Father

Let's look at the boy partner first. *On the surface* he appears to be relatively "harmless." Perhaps he has learned to show gentle sensitivity or perhaps he retreats quickly to his inner world when threatened. Perhaps he has learned to be charming and has found ways to seduce people into thinking highly of him. All these strategies enable him to get by in the world (up to a point, anyway), and they may enable him to move through the early parts of a relationship—until sustained intimacy requires more of him.

However *beneath the surface*, in his shadow side, the boy type is a controlling father who rivals the most extreme father type in intensity! Go deeper than the boy-face he puts on and one discovers a cold, critical, judgmental father type who secretly sets himself up as "better than," the one who really knows best! He has denied this part of himself because it would severely contradict the self-image he has built up— after all, he is certainly not the way his own father was!

The son type often tries very hard to hide this shadow aspect (even from himself) but his intimates always get to experience it in one form or another! For example, in the discussion of mother-son dynamics, we saw that Jim appeared to be a friendly guy to those around him, though his shadow aspect slipped out as caustic, verbal snipes. Nathan appeared to be charming on the outside but under those surface appearances, he had a critical judge who was always covertly (and sometimes overtly) telling his partner she was not good enough for him.

A woman, matched with a son type who disguises or denies his shadow side, often ends up feeling she must be crazy. On the surface, the son partner might appear to be gentle, sensitive, cooperative and/or non-threatening. He certainly shows that mask (often very convincingly) to others around them. But with her, he can be cold and stubborn. He may erupt with strong, angry outbursts that seem to emerge from nowhere. She gets the sense that her imperfections are being constantly judged and yet he won't take responsibility for his judgments (and may even pretend he is unusually accepting).

How does this shadow-parent side of a son type get used in the ongoing battle for control? First, the boy type gets tired of feeling like a powerless child relative to his controlling mother partner. He doesn't know how to deal with her head-on. His shadow-parent part starts to emerge. He has an outburst of anger. Perhaps he becomes a judgmental father and criticizes her for not being good enough. His judgment gets directed to the areas where his partner is most vulnerable, which often have to do with her body (he can always find something wrong) or another important aspect of her feminine being, like her sexuality.

As we have already seen, underneath her controlling mother facade, the mother type is really just a weak little girl who doesn't know who she is. When he adopts the role of controlling father, she is likely to drop into the daughter role for a period of time. For example, when he has outbursts of anger, she might become the placating child. He criticizes her body (or anything else that's important to her) and she collapses into self-castigation. While the boy type sits in his judge, he is on top. He has the control.

His partner doesn't experience being the daughter too long (it might only be seconds) before she, once again, assumes the mother role and finds ways that her partner needs to change. She speaks for him. She corrects him. She'll make herself indispensable. She'll do anything to reclaim the mother position so she won't have to become aware of how powerless and empty she feels inside. Now, playing the mother role again, she is on top. Then he "smells" mother, which triggers his psyche and, being unconscious and not in control of all this, he soon finds himself back to being the reactive child relative to her.

So, the dance goes like this: the son part of a man gets tired of being in his child and moves into "parent" by judging his partner or using some other strategy to undermine her, dropping her into a daughter role. She doesn't want to experience how small she really is and certainly doesn't want to feel less-than, so she moves back to the mother role in order to get control. He does not want to feel less-than when the controlling mother starts to come after him. Rather than feeling his own sense of inadequacy, he tries to take on the parent role and attempts to shift the focus toward her areas of inadequacy, trying to get back "on top." Back and forth it goes. It's like a seesaw, and sometimes the movements occur with dizzying speed. When bonding patterns are present, the times when the seesaw is horizontal—when power is shared equally—are rare.

This dance for control we've been tracing in a mother-son bonding pattern already gives us a preview of what we will find in a father-daughter situation. Even though the fundamentals are the same, there are variations in the steps.

The Daughter Type Becomes a Mother

Like the son type, the woman who habitually plays out the daughter role *appears* to be relatively "harmless." She is likely to show many of the features our culture has associated with the ideal feminine. And that shouldn't be surprising, because the daughter type has decided to play the game with a vengeance. She can masterfully execute the role of a compliant, supportive, agreeable, charming woman. Her feelings of power come from being attractive and she spends huge amounts of her time focusing on her appearance. To her, power is often unconsciously equated with thinness, so her diet becomes a central focus. Successfully applied, her approach to life might help her get places where she seems to be admired by others but it doesn't work very well in sustaining deeper intimacy.

Because everything is based on image for the daughter type, she feels inwardly empty and ineffectual as a woman. She seeks out a powerful man whom she senses will help fill this emptiness and make her feel more like a real woman. At first she is delighted to find him—as she has, of course, found a man who wants to play out a father role. After she gets in deeper with this man, however, if she is honest with herself, she will acknowledge feeling increasingly dissatisfied, though people around her who are also easily impressed by image frequently tell her how lucky she is to be in such a "perfect" relationship. With this man, underneath it all, she finds her feelings of powerlessness and emptiness increasing instead of decreasing.

When the daughter type begins to recognize these feelings (or gets overwhelmed by them), she finds herself confounded. She isn't fulfilled as a woman when she stays in a powerless position relative to her partner, yet she senses that the success of an enduring father-daughter relationship depends on her "knowing her place" and not challenging her father type partner.

116

Any woman who is in touch with herself will feel anger about this and start to express it. The good daughter, however, has learned to cover over her feelings in favor of pleasing others and thus does not really allow herself to feel what is going on inside. She ends up feeling constricted.

Of course, the daughter type has a shadow side, too! Go deeper than the girl-face she puts on and one finds a cold, controlling, critical mother who secretly sees herself as the most special of special. This is the part she doesn't want to know about herself, because it would contradict the self-image she wants to hold. (We can also surmise that at least part of this shadow side of hers would remind her too much of her own mother!)

As the relationship progresses, she recognizes that her father partner is really just a puffed up version of a needy, egocentric boy. His cover might be extremely thick, but she recognizes that underneath it, he is vulnerable to criticism. Because he is fearful of the feminine, if she can establish a controlling mother role that will get through his defenses, he will collapse into his boy part.

Let's look at an example of this step in the dance for control. The daughter part of a woman gets tired of being the powerless member in the relationship and brings out her critical mother. She judges him for not being good enough and does it in a big way. In spite of whatever he does, she is clear that he can never do it well enough for her. When she is successful in this strategy, he drops off his perch and becomes the boy; while this is going on, she is on top.

The father part of a man, abhorring feeling powerless, will need to do something to regain his power. Different men use different strategies to regain power. Some "fathers" use impressive, rational words to prove she is "the problem." Others use their financial clout to remind her who is boss. Still others call upon their physical presence to establish dominance. Whatever way is used, he gets back on top and reestablishes her as the daughter again. But . . . the daughter doesn't like feeling powerless and goes back to critical mother to diminish him. And on and on and on we go.

Summary of the Dance for Control

Laying out the steps of the struggle for control in this fashion may seem a little absurd, but *these are the things that happen in relationship.* Actually, the whole struggle for control is absurd, because a huge amount of a couple's energy is used up in this invisible dance and neither partner gets his or her needs met in fully satisfying ways.

Often the parent type is less aware than the child type of, or perhaps is even oblivious to, the intensity of the struggle for control and power. Mother and father types are accustomed to assuming they have the control and their having it seems only natural to them. With great tenacity, they persist in the view that their partner is less mature or more in need of their guidance. Of course. That's just how things are.

On the other side of the equation, the determination of the child type to gain a sense of power or control in relationship, regardless of the cost, can hardly be overstated. Every day in our practice, Naomi and I see child types who would rather sacrifice their emotional and/or sexual well-being than let their parent partner have a sense of control. The preservation of their soul would seem to be at stake. The motto of the child type ought to be "Death before Surrender," or perhaps more accurately, "Deadness before Surrender."

Clearly, this struggle for control is ultimately destructive to both parties, yet the pattern we have been describing is common and pervasive in intimate relationships. Its roots run deep and, from what Naomi and I have seen, Band-Aid compromises just don't work over the long run. In order for healing shifts to occur, both partners must be willing to look into their own inner being and to address the pattern at the root level.

While keeping in mind that no simple or exact answers are to be found, let's look at a few general similarities in the backgrounds of individuals who get caught in bonding patterns, then try to develop an understanding of how they evolve the way they do.

THE EVOLUTION OF PARENT AND CHILD TYPES
Parent Types

Frequently, individuals who instinctively adopt parent roles were raised in a situation where they needed to grow up fast. In some ways, they were expected to take on the role of "adult" in the family constellation and were not allowed just to be children. The fastest way to "mature" was to put on an adult facade and the chances are that they were rewarded for doing so. But taking on a facade does not eliminate the child underneath; it only covers the child over. (One of John Bradshaw's powerful truisms is that the child who is not allowed to be a child has a tendency to stay a child forever, regardless of what mask is developed.) Parent types, upon becoming adults, have long since adapted to this situation. The feelings that arose when, as children, they were pressured into adult responsibilities before they were ready have long been forgotten or repressed.

The process of learning to show an adult mask in the earliest years often proves to be beneficial during young to middle adulthood. Individuals in these age categories are often able to get a faster start in life. They achieve some early positive recognition by others, which helps them build a more positive self-image. What they do not realize is that the image they learn to uphold is often separate from the feelings they experience beneath the surface. Their adult mask will also interfere with intimate relating, where vulnerability, feelings, and equal sharing are required.

What happens for them when they are with intimate partners? Parent types learned early on that in order to have an identity and be recognized, they need to care for and support the opposite sex. In their construction of reality, this is the way a person needs to be in order to gain closeness to others, to be in intimacy. It's easiest to see in the mother type so let's look at her first.

Mother Type

The extreme mother type probably grew up believing she needed to take care of things in the family. Her father is likely to have been blocked emotionally (or absent altogether) and though he may have looked like a mature adult, especially in her eyes, he was probably quite a child underneath the surface. Her own mother was likely not able (or refused) to fully meet her father's emotional needs and she felt she needed to be the one to really care for him. She formed the idea at a very early age that all men need mothering and that the way to be with them is to "be a mother."

Taking on the mother role serves her reasonably well in the first half of life. In chapter 6, we looked at how the mother role gives her an identity, a way of being that is accepted and approved of by others. It also provides her a way of defending against her own feelings of being a needy, powerless child inside. In addition, it provides her with a way of experiencing a sense of power; and, given that there is no shortage of men who are secretly looking for a mother, it generally is an effective strategy for attracting them.

In sustained intimate relationships, however, the mother role is deadly. First off, she is defended against her more vulnerable feelings and has great difficulty sharing the vulnerable part of herself with her partner. Intimacy is blocked. Surrender to the masculine is next to impossible, as mother types are always on guard. In order to sustain the mother role, she needs to have a partner who is powerless, who needs to be rescued, who is a victim.

The mother type is only going to attract boy types, and as she goes into the second half of life, she is truly disgusted with them! She wants a *man*, but because she is unconscious of her own role, she can't figure out why she keeps ending up with boys (or is alone). A man who is reasonably integrated avoids her, because he can see how controlling she is. Father types avoid her like the plague because no one can see an imposter like another imposter!

Father Type

Most of what has been said about the mother type also applies to the father type. Early in his family experience, he learned to take on a mature facade. In his eyes now, his mother might be the greatest human being who ever lived, but she was probably very much a child beneath her cover and looked for him to be an adult. Her needs were probably not getting met by her husband and this future father type was expected to provide what she lacked in terms of emotional support.

At an early age he formed the idea that women are like children. The way to be with them is to take care of them and offer support. Later on in life, with this deeply ingrained attitude, he discovers that finding partners is relatively easy, but sustaining deeper intimacy is problematic and he has difficulty understanding why that is so.

He gets confused because taking on the father role serves him well in the other areas of his life. In addition to giving himself an identity, he gets cultural recognition and respect because the characteristics of "father" are highly valued. This cultural acceptance makes it easier for him to defend against his inner feelings and gives him tacit support for not going inward. He also attracts many women, as they rush to a man who provides the father qualities he seems to offer.

Deeper intimacy requires individuals who are willing to go inward and be vulnerable. The staunch father type is defended against his more vulnerable feelings and has no desire whatsoever to go back and experience how young he really feels underneath his cover. With his intimate partner, his instinct is often to jockey to a position where he demolishes her boundaries and practically takes over her life. His need to continually keep up a facade of power also means he has great difficulty receiving in a genuine way. If, therefore, he only supports and can't receive, he ends up feeling depleted, unable to give authentically. Most difficult of all, the father type, in order to keep up the game, needs a partner who is continually powerless. All this does not lead to a mutually fulfilling relationship over the long term.

Child Types

Individuals who habitually act out the child role in relationship frequently grew up in what might be considered an overprotected environment. The real power in their household was probably held by the opposite-sex parent. In their early family experiences, child types are likely to have had a strong bond with that opposite-sex parent and/or they grew up somewhat distanced from their same-sex parent. For example, the daughter type is determined not to grow up to be like her mother. Similarly, the son type secretly vows not to grow up to be like his father. The result is simply that neither of them ever grows up!

Daughter Type

As she develops in life, whether she admits it to herself or not, the daughter type attributes all power to the masculine. At the same time, she doesn't have a particularly high view of her mother and the feminine side of things. She downgrades her own feminine and orients her life around becoming attractive to men because of her perception that they have the power.

Taking on the daughter role serves her reasonably well in the first half of life. A successful daughter type receives cultural approval and is sought after by men. Many of society's doors are opened to her if she plays the game well enough. People are, in general, drawn to her apparent vulnerability. Individuals who live on the surface of things even hold her up as being the ideal feminine.

After she has entered into intimate relationship, however, the daughter type has problems. To maintain her relationship as it was established, she needs to remain powerless. But this is a big problem for her because of something important we haven't mentioned yet. The shadow side of the daughter type is her hunger for power. Below her good daughter facade, she is controlling and will manipulate in any way she can to have power! She is able to maneuver better than any controlling mother type, and she is using her powerful partner just as much as he is using her.

This need for power by the daughter type is a big part of her shadow side and if she doesn't bring it out into the open at some point in her life, her only choice is to wither away. This leads to a major dilemma for her. If she doesn't come out, she withers, but if she does come out with her need for power, she will probably be rejected by her partner, who needs her to be powerless in order to keep up *his* facade. And, being still very much in her child, she does not feel she will be able to go into the world and make it on her own if he were to reject her.

After the romantic phase is over, she has yet another problem. She discovers that, underneath his posturing, her powerful father type partner is really just a needy little boy, who feels even more unworthy than she does. He really needs a mother but she is supposed to be the daughter, not his mother! Her expectations of being cared for by the ideal masculine of her dreams show less and less promise of being fulfilled. This is very disappointing and depressing for her. Sometimes she reaches the point where she can't even shop her blues away.

Son Type

Most of what is true for the daughter part of a woman is also true for the son part of a man. As we have seen many times heretofore, whether he admits it or not, the feminine is very big in his eyes. In most cases he grew up strongly bonded with his mother and saw her as the ideal. His mother probably held the real power in the household and he believes his father was a lesser force in his life. If his mother left him at an early age or if she was not large enough to meet his ideal, he is likely to have created a fantasy relationship with her in his own mind.

By most definitions, the son role serves him only moderately well in the first half of life. Unless he finds a good way to capitalize on his boy nature, he doesn't tend to make a very good living for himself. Relationships, though, are relatively easy to find because he does seem to understand women. However, son types who enter into relationship discover that sustaining intimacy isn't easy. Either they experience a fast

123

turnover of short-term, seduction-based relationships or they find themselves locking horns with a controlling mother type.

As we've noted many times already, the son type doesn't want to see himself as he really is and has a strong tendency to remain unaware of his true nature by closing off emotionally and retreating into his own mind, refusing to feel anything. Part of what he does is to have a fantasy relationship with an ideal woman who never quite arrives in flesh-and-blood terms, and if she does arrive, she never stays too long. Thus, he is able to remain aloof (and continue to feel special). If he does enter a longer relationship with a real, live partner, he experiences disappointment that she is never quite good enough.

After a while into his relationship with a mother type, he begins to recognize that his partner, underneath her cover, is really just a needy little girl who feels very unworthy. Being emotionally young himself, he doesn't feel capable of caring for her and, though the prospect doesn't hold the promise of being expansive for him, he would rather that she carry on as the mother. He is numb and disappointed, but remains in the relationship because, as a boy, he is terrified of stepping out into the world on his own. Many son types make frequent visits to the lottery vendor hoping for a ticket out of their situation. Others develop a substitute love-relationship with their computer.

The Challenge for Bonded Partners

The challenge is clear. Bonded partners need to understand something about the underlying dynamics of their relationship. They must let go of the images they have created of themselves and refrain from the posturing they do to sustain the images—at least long enough to begin grappling with the feelings running under the surface. They need to get big enough to uncover their shadow side. In short, they need to become more conscious.

Saying it is easy, but how do they go about doing it? These individuals all have someone right in front of them who is fully capable of enlightening them. Their partner. Their partner is showing them parts of themselves they refuse to accept. Their partner has already developed what they need to incorporate into themselves in order to become more whole and mature. *Instead of competing for control and starving each other out, the partners could use each other as teachers.*

How might this work?

Awareness that the Parent Type Needs

Many times in this book, we have seen that partners who habitually act out the parental role have difficulty coping with their powerless and needy inner parts. In fact, their mask has been developed as a defense against these parts; they want to show the world they *are not* powerless or needy. Yet they find themselves with a partner who is powerless and needy.

In the earlier stages of relationship, they are attracted to this powerless partner because, to a significant degree, that partner affords them the opportunity to keep their own "powerful" mask on, to play out their role. Later on, as they get but little in return or find themselves being diminished by their "powerless" partner, they start to push away.

When this pushing away begins to happen in a relationship, as it inevitably will, a choice point arrives. They can try to get their partner to change. They can continue retreating until a crisis emerges or numbness sets in. Or they can look inward to find out what is happening.

The first strategy is doomed to failure. Naomi and I have found that lasting change in intimate relationship doesn't usually take hold unless both partners are willing to change in equal proportion. The second strategy feels safer at first, but will eventually lead to pain, even if it is the final pain of a deadened relationship or of life only partially lived. The third strategy, though much more difficult, stands a chance of producing life-enhancing results, including a revitalized intimacy.

Parent types need to learn that their child partner is acting out a part of *themselves* they have generally denied, a part of themselves they need to reclaim if they are going to experience wholeness and genuine maturity. For example, the father type sees a partner who has feelings of fear, unworthiness, neediness, vulnerability, anger, and powerlessness. *These are the very feelings he needs to locate inside himself* if he is to become aware of who he is beneath his mask and ultimately grow into his authentic, mature masculine. He needs to shift from mastering the outer world to understanding the inner, feeling world.

A man who likes to act out the parent type will balk at this prescription. What is the value of becoming vulnerable in such a way? What is the value of knowing fear and feelings of unworthiness? Of what possible value could powerlessness be for a person who wants to feel powerful? So let's go a little farther with this idea and use powerlessness as an example.

Power Versus Powerlessness

In our culture, showing power is, in general, judged favorably, whereas showing powerlessness is something to be avoided. Powerlessness is equated with weakness of character, with failure to achieve, with incompetence, with defeat. Men have special difficulty seeing value in powerlessness, though women who have been taught to strive for power have no less difficulty.

In line with this premise, we can see clearly that anytime we are so unfortunate as to find ourselves powerless, we regard it as being a problem. And then we strive quickly and by any means possible to rectify that problem and become powerful again. This general *need for power* then (and naturally enough) gets carried into intimate relationships, where each person strives to maintain a power position relative to his or her partner.

But here's the kicker: nature dictates that life must sooner or later come into balance. Each person carries the potential for living out the full spectrum of the human drama. In ordinary life, feelings of power need to be balanced by feelings of powerlessness and vulnerability. In spite of what the ego-self might want to believe, you can't have one without the other. Only in mythology or idealization can someone be identified exclusively with power. Attempting to hold on to the stance of power is costly, and people who insist on maintaining *only* power eventually come to their knees and experience powerlessness in spite of their endeavors. (The image of Howard Hughes comes to mind.)

In order to avoid feelings of powerlessness, individuals must continuingly be separate, on guard, and struggling for control. In defending against their feelings of powerlessness, they are forever in judgment, assessing the power of those around them. People who live this life are in constant rejection. Anyone perceived as less powerful may be tolerated on the surface but is deemed insignificant and ultimately rejected. Anyone perceived as more powerful is to be avoided, idealized, used, or conquered—all of which are also forms of rejection. Avoiding feelings of powerlessness narrows the possibilities for intimacy down considerably.

Not only is much energy consumed in denial, judgment, and rejection, but people who will not accept their powerlessness also have no chance of accepting themselves in their totality. They are constantly saying to themselves: "I don't want to feel powerless; I don't want to feel powerless." But the truth is that part of them *is* powerless. Thus they are saying in essence, "I don't want to be who I am; I don't want to be who I am." The irony here is that individuals who refuse to be who they are and who thus live in delusion about themselves can *never* have their full power available to them. They only have an image of power, which will break down sooner or later when they run out of energy to sustain (or enforce) it.

In terms of our examination of personal relationship, the most important spinoff of these understandings is that individuals who don't know who they are and live in delusion about themselves cannot hope to experience a fulfilling intimate life. Nobody is really "home." They must be inside themselves and know who they are before they can truly give of themselves to, or receive from, another person. A man who lives in the delusion of only showing power and avoiding powerlessness lives life avoiding half of himself. A man who lives avoiding half of himself cannot demonstrate the full adult masculine; he can only construct an image of it—of what he thinks it should be—and display it as a facade, the way an actor plays a role. His partner, however, is there to teach him about these inner parts of himself if he is willing to learn.

Similarly, the mother type needs to understand that her boy type partner is present in her life to remind her about parts of herself she does not want to accept. His powerlessness and emotional immaturity are a reflection back to her of how *she* really feels inside. The way he closes off emotionally is a reflection of how closed and self-protected she really is. His defensiveness is a reflection of how walled-off she is.

For parent types, going "inside" requires a lot more vulnerability than they generally feel comfortable with. They encounter too many feelings left over from early childhood, feelings they don't want to know about. They have spent a lifetime pushing these feelings down, and allowing them to come up now threatens their construct of reality. They prefer to invent a thousand reasons to justify not going inward: they are too busy for feelings; feelings are useless (or are the domain of the child); therapy is self-indulgent and only for individuals who are afraid of life.

Awareness that the Child Type Needs

Child types may have a better grasp on the inner world (they usually spend more time there) but they have a lot to learn about who they are. Their parent partner is only reflecting back their own denied parts. For example, the son type, in seeing a partner who is critical, controlling, condescending, angry, dominating, and hungry for power, is seeing the underside of himself. The sooner he starts becoming aware of these parts of his shadow, the sooner he can emerge from behind his wall of protection and discover who he really is. The son type needs to wake up from his delusion—to take heed of his partner's demand to grow up and do something with his life, to face his feelings of powerlessness and grandiosity, to step out and seek his power in the world—before he has any chance of moving into a more mature masculine.

The daughter type needs to see that her condescending, competitive, power-seeking partner is really showing her parts of herself she doesn't want to see. She was drawn to her parent partner because she wanted for herself the type of power he shows. Thus, instead of pushing him away or attempting to bring him down to her size, she needs to internalize him and bring into herself what he already has. The power she needs to bring forth in order to move into a more mature feminine is already present in her own shadow side if she is willing to go there and retrieve it.

While we are discussing what the child type needs to learn, let us digress for a moment to look at a lesson which the "son" in every man needs to learn. We have seen that the son part of a man is very critical beneath the surface. We have seen how his critical parent comes out to defend against his feelings of powerlessness, hoping to balance the power in the relationship. We have also seen that a common way for the boy part of a man to make himself feel more powerful is to criticize his partner's body.

Not for a long time did I recognize that my own inclination to judge and criticize came up most strongly when I was feeling the most powerless and inadequate—and did not want to acknowledge it to myself. This wasn't a conscious process on my part. I would just find myself obsessing about how my partner wasn't "measuring up." As I focused on her, judging her against an ideal which couldn't possibly be attained, I could avoid looking at what was really happening within myself. These days, when I feel the urge to criticize, I stop and take a closer look at what is going on within me. I've been amazed by the discoveries I've made.

For many years, Naomi played into this game as well. She also bought into this ideal and would collapse almost immediately when my body-critic emerged. I didn't even have to say anything aloud and she would react! The power-hungry part of me was glad she collapsed so easily; but really, how can one have a fulfilling relationship with a collapsed person? (Actually, both people are collapsed.)

This whole charade is widespread and deeply enmeshed in our culture; its impact on the collective feminine is profound. Men and women both share a role in keeping it going. When, I wonder, are we going to wake up and discover that neither sex comes out nourished by it in the long run?

Nor is this only a one-sided phenomenon. Women also have a strong tendency to bash their partners when they are really just feeling lousy about themselves.

The Need for Help

Intellectually acknowledging that feelings exist below the surface in bonded individuals is not sufficient to produce much useful change. Denied feelings need to be *felt*, not *thought*. Individuals who cannot *feel* their feelings are blocked from access to an essential part of the self and cannot know who they really are in the fullest sense.

Similarly, a rational understanding that their partners represent hidden parts of themselves, parts they need to incorporate into themselves in order to be whole, is seldom sufficient to bring forth much real change. Partners caught in bonding patterns generally have a long history of control struggles, and their suddenly being able to see a partner as an ally and teacher does not happen easily. Resentments and anger have built up. Habitual (mostly unconscious) behavior patterns tend to take over automatically. Partners are hyper-alert to control attempts from the other and are ready to bring up defenses and dysfunctional strategies in the blink of an eye.

Thus, the matter of therapeutic assistance emerges. But shouldn't everyone be able to find and express hidden feelings without therapeutic help? The truth is that most people don't. When a lot of painful history exists in a relationship, a neutral, clear-minded, dispassionate observer who is respected by both parties can be of great assistance. Hiring someone who has the appropriate therapeutic expertise can greatly accelerate movement toward a more functional, vital relationship.

130

"What you can feel, you can heal. What you can't, you won't."
—from *Vancouver M.E.N.* magazine

The Consequences of Not Taking Up the Challenge
When bonding patterns are not dealt with and a couple remains stuck in control struggles, the consequences are not pretty. Such a relationship, once it gets going, is resilient. The couple can be functional during their twenties and thirties, though the tendency is to fall into a brother-sister relationship, where both partners are good friends (at best) but without much passion. Though they experience little fulfillment as men and women, both are afraid of striking out on their own.

Let's take a look first at partners who are stuck in a mother-son bonding pattern. When the participants in a mother-son type of relationship approach midlife, the sparks often begin to fly. Perhaps the woman gets tired of being with a collapsed boy or the man gets tired of being with such a controlling mother. Everything is the other person's fault, of course. Accepting any blame would be like losing control and neither partner is willing to do that! Each partner builds an almost impregnable defense—often giving just enough to keep the relationship from collapsing. Both are angry. Neither, however, is willing to deal with the anger openly.

Both partners end up feeling disappointed and hopeless, because that (stubborn, unconscious) partner just can't be changed, just won't grow up. Some relationships fall apart at this point; others start the long slide into resignation: he closes off his emotions, she closes sexually and numbs to him. Though they tolerate each other, both partners feel undernourished. They use their kids to make up for deficiencies in the bond with each other.

Occasionally there are affairs. The seducer boy-type might go from woman to woman until his game (or his body) gets old. Or, if he doesn't act the seduction out, the younger boy-type often persists with an ideal fantasy-lover in his mind, which has much of the same impact on his relationship as an actual lover. Even the younger mother-type might have a fling, but the chances are that she will become wrapped up in her family (where she can mother the kids to the point that they can't breathe).

In the household, the woman becomes increasingly dominant as the years go by, while the son-type man, who refuses to take the challenge of finding himself and growing up, fades into the background of the family. (One finds no shortage of old son-types who sit in the background watching TV or reading the newspaper while their wives do the talking for them.)

By way of comparison, how do the stuck father-daughter bonding patterns fare? The extreme father-daughter partners are often viewed as the model couple by those around them. Inside the relationship, the egocentricity of the father type prevails and he tends to get his way (or so he thinks). The daughter type plays the game up to the point where she begins to experience an urge to move into a more mature, balanced feminine.

Does she come forth and risk the relationship or does she opt to stay in the shadow of his power? Her anger at the situation builds, but being a daughter type, she is very uncomfortable with anger. She doesn't even want to become aware of her feelings of powerlessness. As time goes by, she feels increasingly unhappy but may even experience guilt about that, because things look so good on the surface.

The extreme father type will hardly even notice how unhappy she is, but if he does, he will be oriented toward looking for solutions to her problems. Go to a psychiatrist, find the right medication, take a holiday, arrange for cosmetic surgery, buy something new. Meanwhile, as she closes herself off, he is increasingly aware of being shut out. He feels hurt, punished, underfed, and angry but is unwilling to admit to having these feelings because he won't admit to experiencing vulnerability.

Eventually she reaches a point where she needs to decide either to go for her own power separate from him—or resign herself to the status quo. Going for her power means upping the stakes. In the extreme situation, she threatens to leave or finds a lover. Sometimes she does manage to shake things up and evoke a positive outcome, though her challenge may be the beginning of the end. If she decides to opt for the status quo, the slide into resignation begins.

The father type finds himself confused by all of this. He believes he is doing everything right. But he can't avoid recognizing that most of the passion has left his marriage. Some "fathers" just decide to make the best of it, often becoming increasingly rigid as they grow older. Other incorrigible father types discover that a new and even more vibrant daughter type is interested, and off they go.

The father type left with a daughter type who refuses to grow up is not likely to expand much as the years go by. He got what he wanted but not what he really wanted! Having lived a life cut off from his feelings, he won't even acknowledge his unhappiness. He is reluctant to step out of his groove and try new experiences. Even if he were willing to open up a little, he doesn't believe his self-centered daughter-woman is really capable of supporting him in his vulnerability. He gets to hold on to his facade, but both end up going to their graves emotionally underdeveloped and relatively unconscious of who they really are.

The eventual outcome for individuals caught in bonding patterns over the long term is shared by all types. As old age comes along, the "children" they have always been beneath their masks become increasingly evident. Rather than taking their place as elders and guiding society with their wisdom, they abandon responsibility, perhaps complaining about lack of respect from the younger generation. The anger they have withheld throughout their life often shows in the rigid, narrow viewpoints they adopt. As opposed to contributing to their society in meaningful and powerful ways, they opt instead for self-absorption, self-protection, and collapse.

Not Merely Personal—A Wider Perspective

We have seen how damaging the unconscious emotional child can be in relationship, but let's not ignore the larger-scale impact of this immature inner aspect. In our society, the evidence of collective immaturity is all around us and we have now reached the point where coming to terms with this phony inner adult is crucial.

Only an infantile consciousness would burn up and cut down vital resources with wild abandon or go into crippling debt with little thought for future consequences. Only a young mentality would leave toxic materials in its wake and not expect to pay dearly somewhere down the line. Only the immature are easily seduced by images and would elect their leaders accordingly. Only adolescents would reward professional athletes with the highest status and pay, while the public school systems go begging for funds. It is the adolescent mentality that gets a thrill out of delivering mayhem to people across an ocean merely to support the image of "decisive" leadership. Only a very young society would allow destruction of its economic infrastructure so a relative few could accumulate far more than they might ever sensibly use. And on it goes.

If we are to change any of this, we must ask ourselves if we are willing to become aware of the child part within and begin collectively to grow up. Our doing so starts by knowing the self, because persons who do not know who they really are cannot be counted upon to give the reliable guidance and support our society desperately needs at this time. If we don't take up this challenge, our children are going to have to pay a painful price.

Coming Up:

Couples stuck in bonding patterns tend to justify their life of resignation with each other by telling themselves they are staying together "for the sake of the children." Perhaps their doing so is good, but they may also need to recognize that the children who are saved are also sacrificed. Children become the scapegoats as the dysfunctional patterns continue, and they end up carrying a heavy load as a result. Not having had emotionally mature adults to parent them, children later relive the same dysfunction in intimacy as their parents did. The next chapter will explore this important and disturbing tendency.

9

WHEN TWO CHILDREN HAVE A BABY

Even though all relationships have some measure of both mother-son and father-daughter relating patterns, we have made a sharp distinction between them and treated them separately in order to organize our analysis. Now, as we are beginning to understand that these patterns stem from the same root, we are able to let go of that distinction altogether and simply deal with *bonded couples* (as we shall call them). We will explore the ways in which all bonded couples wound their children and plant the seeds for later dysfunction in intimate relationship.

In the last chapter, we saw that bonded couples find themselves locked into roles with each other which neither partner finds very fulfilling. We came to recognize how both partners have difficulty seeing themselves clearly and how they really don't know themselves outside of the roles they learned to play early in their lives. Both experience disappointment in relationship because they expected more from intimacy than what they got. At the same time, they both feel dependent on one another and are unwilling to end the relationship. One could say they have ended up with a "stalemate."

When the urge to bear children surfaces, a couple often has an unspoken expectation that a child will revive their relationship—and many times the arrival of a child does give the relationship a boost for a period of time. Unfortunately, a child cannot heal a relationship that is locked in bonding patterns. In fact, all too often, the children become the casualties in this type of relationship.

The topic we are about to delve into is potentially explosive because, while Naomi and I have noticed that bonded couples will endure all manner of frustrations and deprivations in their relationship with each other, the children are sacred. For a father and mother to accept that their relationship with the children has a shadow side is extremely difficult.

In the model we will present, we do not pretend to have definitive truths that will hold firm in all circumstances. The behaviors and patternings of human beings are much too complicated to capture in a few words. Our intent is, in general, simply to evoke awareness and stimulate different ways of looking at child rearing.

OVERBONDING

Bonded couples make up for the deficiencies in their relationship by forming special alliances with their children. These alliances go past healthy bonding and become what we will call "overbonding." In an overbonded situation, the child becomes the center of focus for the parent. The parent looks for the child to meet intimacy needs and to fill his or her sense of inner emptiness. The parent becomes over-involved with the child and unconsciously pressures the child to accomplish what the parent, for whatever reason, didn't. In fact, the child gets *used*. To understand this a little better, let's look at the situation when a baby arrives.

A Baby Arrives to Bonded Parents

Imagine for a moment being a child who has just arrived to a couple caught up in bonding patterns.

The parents are disappointed with each other. Under the surface, both are angry about being stuck for a lifetime with a cold, stubborn, immature, rejecting partner who is always struggling for control. Though neither of them wants to admit to it, both feel empty and unfulfilled inside. In fact, both parents are really just needy children beneath their facades.

You, this imaginary child, are now given the responsibility of providing your parents with a reason for staying in their relationship with each other. Being empty and unfulfilled, they look to you to give them a sense of purpose. As they are not nourishing each other, you are expected to offer them the emotional warmth they are not getting. They see you as part of themselves and are willing to be vulnerable with you. However, they do not see *each other* as part of themselves and, in fact, are engaged in a deadlocked struggle with each other. They see you as precious and special but look at each other from behind walls of defense and hurt.

Though your physical needs may be well cared for, this is not a situation in which you will simply be allowed to be who you are and grow up naturally in a nurturing, trust-inspiring environment. Your parents are going to use you as a pawn while they struggle through unresolved, unconscious issues with each other. Each parent is going to use you to compensate for deficiencies in his or her own life. (To make matters even more confusing, they are going to do this in the name of "love and caring.")

Given that this is a book about the relationship between the sexes, we will focus special attention on the formative experiences of an infant with his or her opposite-sex parent. This connection sets the stage for all future relations with the opposite sex. So let's start by taking a look at what happens beneath the surface as a mother overbonds with her son. In order to emphasize the generational continuity of bonding patterns, we'll follow this same son through to adulthood to see how he recreates a bonded relationship for himself. We'll see that he will not only have difficulty with intimate relationship but, in turn, will also keep the pattern alive by overbonding with his own daughter.

A Male Child Arrives to Bonded Parents

We have seen that, whether she acts out a mother type or daughter type on the surface, the woman in a bonded relationship is emotionally very young. She eventually realizes that her husband is not the prince she was expecting. She sees her partner as a weak boy type who cannot support her in the way she needs, or as a father type who expects her to be submissive to him so he can feel powerful. In either case, she doesn't feel very fulfilled or expanded by her primary relationship.

Now she gets pregnant.

The typical woman who comes through our office says she never felt as powerful as when she was pregnant. She is creating life itself and has been entrusted with the ultimate responsibility of supporting this life through its formative, most vulnerable stage. She experiences being in her body in a way she never has before. She experiences her feelings in an authentic way that can't be denied. She gets attention and is acknowledged by those around her for her femininity. This mixture of having a sense of purpose and being acknowledged by others helps her feel particularly worthwhile. She gets a taste of what being in her fuller feminine is like, and it is a potent experience.

The child is born. The duties begin. The attention she received before now shifts to the baby. Because her feeling self, strongly stimulated during pregnancy, is still active, her sense of emptiness and powerlessness (which she always had but usually pushed away) often emerges with uncomfortable intensity. If she wants to avoid these feelings, one way to do it is to take on motherhood with a vengeance! She finds meaning by becoming a "super mother" for her child. The net result is that she uses her child to give herself an identity, to fill the emptiness she feels within.

When the child is a son, many powerful forces are set into motion. On the conscious level, more often than not, an empty mother tells herself she is going to be the best mother a son ever had. He will be so loved by her that he will grow up to be healthy and strong. Though her husband is something of a "dud," this male child of hers will not be; he will make a real contribution to the world.

A number of unconscious processes are also predictable at this time. To the degree that she is unhappy with her partner, this mother places an expectation on her son to fill the void her husband has not been able to fill. She also feels as though the inner emptiness she experiences can somehow be healed by her child. Unconsciously, therefore, her child becomes a symbol for her, the one who will somehow embody the power that eluded her. She begins to associate her own feelings of efficacy and worthiness with the "performance" of her child. Because, deep down, she wants to feel special herself, she needs to have a *very* special boy to accomplish this task.

In order for him to be the most special of all, the overbonded mother is willing to sacrifice herself. She gives herself away to make sure everything is right for her son. She hovers over him and obsesses about his well-being. She over-protects him from many of life's experiences. She has great difficulty turning over care to anyone else and is totally convinced her child can't bear being without her when, in fact, it is really she who needs him.

Generally speaking, two typical unconscious responses emerge from the male child who is implicitly expected to fill his mother's emotional needs and live vicariously for her. One is something like: "No problem, Mom. I'll get out there and do it for you. And I'll do it perfectly. I'll get the power for you. In fact, I'll do it right now and start being an adult for you. I'll heal you (and every other powerless woman) by bringing power and meaning to you (and them)." The father type is born!

The other response tends to embody a little more wariness:"Hey, this is too much for me. I'm just a kid. I don't want to do it anyway, because I couldn't do it as perfectly as you expect. I'm not going to do it and, in fact, I'm not going to do *anything* until you care for and support me like I really need. If I heed your demands, my soul, that which is distinctly me, could be swallowed up. I sense there is no bottom to your well of neediness and as much as I would like to heal you, I need to close off and withdraw." The son type is born!

This hypothetical internal "self-talk" is a little over-dramatic, but from it one can get a sense of the stress a male child experiences when faced with these hidden but immensely potent demands from his overbonded mother. His psyche takes in the impression that the feminine is demanding and filled with very big expectations. The feminine expects him to *do* something for her and does not just accept him for who he is. He learns that he needs to be alert to protecting himself from such a potentially consuming force if he is to retain any sense of self, separate from her. The survival of his soul depends on finding ways to keep her at arm's length.

At the same time, the male child also feels a strong urge to comply with his mother's wishes. At the most basic level, his survival depends on her. He experiences huge fear of not living up to her expectations. Deep down, he is terrified of incurring her anger. He also wants to please. He wants to heal her. The seeds of a lifelong inner ambivalence about the feminine are sown!

On the one hand, the son feels dependent and small around his mother. On the other, he feels important and special. If his mother needs him in order to define herself, to justify her existence, he is put into a very powerful role. However, just as her expectations are too much for him at such an early age, the power she confers upon him in this way also will bring him problems. So let's look at the shadow side of this process.

When overbonding exists between mother and son, an implicit agreement or collusion is present under the surface. Beneath all of her perfect-mother behavior, she is unconsciously saying to her son, "Let's make a pact. I'll promote you and see you as the most special of all for the rest of your life, and you give me a sense of meaning and a purpose for being. I'll care for you completely, even at the expense of myself, and you bring me the tenderness and attention I am missing. I'll make you feel powerful if you bond with me; together, you and I will be a force to be reckoned with." Even children have shadow sides and if he can get power by bonding with her in this fashion, he will.

Of course, some sons collude more than others but, in general, the invitation is a hard one to pass up. He gets to be special and adored. He gets to be the major masculine force in her life. Of course, he is unconscious of all this, and he is also unconscious of the costs of receiving this type of "power" too early.

I was strongly impacted by the pathos of this situation while watching a program on the PBS *Nature* series titled "Monkey Island," about a colony of rhesus monkeys on an island off Puerto Rico.

These monkeys live in hierarchical societies, with an alpha (i.e., dominant) male and female at the top of each group. Part of the film focused on a male offspring of a dominant female who, with his mother's help, was elevated to the position of alpha male in his society at an unusually early age. As an alpha male, he was automatically accorded all the privileges of being the top male—without having had to learn the basics of how to survive in his community.

As it turned out, this young alpha male was unseated from his position at a relatively early age. He ended up spending his remaining days more or less banished, as an outcast, with a small, shabby group of other deposed, ex-alpha males. These outcast males could only exist on the fringe of the society because they hadn't acquired basic social skills and were unable to compete. Clearly, the monkey who is accorded too much specialness too young grows up crippled.

As the human mother overbonds with her male child, he will also pay a cost in terms of his relationship with his father, and ultimately his own adult masculine. As the bond between mother and son increases, the father gradually recedes into the background and gets increasingly excluded from both of their hearts. We must remember that the father in a bonded relationship is also young emotionally and, even though he is being rejected, he often experiences some relief to be left in a world of his own. The pressure is off him—and on his son.

Some extremely overbonded sons demonstrate obvious behavioral problems as they progress through childhood, but for many, the costs are not obvious until later. (Once again all of this is happening at an unconscious level; on the surface, everything seems normal.) In the son's early years, the mother seems to be doing her job well and she might be widely praised, even by her husband. She feels fulfilled by playing her role. The father is doing the best he can.

Let's fast-forward now to puberty for the son. His hormones erupt and he starts to experience sexual urges, which, of course, affect his relationships with his mother and the feminine as a whole. He wants to move toward other women but the pact with his overbonded mother is still intact. All the conflicting emotions that emerge out of this chaotic time are too much for him and, if he hasn't already done so at an earlier stage, he begins a process of closing down emotionally. He separates from his feelings and starts to live life from his rational mind, which is safer and much more manageable!

Learning to live life from his head serves the son. In the world of his rational mind, he can refute the pact with this mother and deny the power that the feminine (represented by his mother) has over him. So he begins to develop his own power, a power based on what he thinks. By living life from his rational mind, he is able to avoid experiencing his feelings. The unfortunate part is that a man who lives life only through what he *thinks* is subject to delusion. In this case, the son is not aware that he is living life protectively, defensively. Rather than recognize that he has closed off a major portion of his feelings, he "thinks" he is conscious of who he is.

Let's review a few of the feelings he has "forgotten," feelings that still exist below the mask he has learned to present to the world. We review them to remind ourselves that these same feelings are the ones he will carry unconsciously into all his relationships with women. These are also feelings that will gradually be evoked by his future partner as he gets deeper into intimacy with her.

He feels *angry* at the feminine for pressuring him into being an adult before his time. He feels *insecure*, because he hasn't ever been totally accepted for just being who he is (a little boy). He feels *fear of being consumed* by the feminine, because his own mother was so hungry and needy. Underneath his mask, even the "best behaved" boy feels *defiance* and determination to preserve some sense of self in the face of a consuming feminine. At the same time, he feels a *need to comply* with the feminine, because his mother was so potent a force in his early life. He feels *fear of being rejected* by the feminine (much more than his rational thoughts would admit to). He also feels *very special* and deserving of adoration by the feminine.

Let's fast-forward once again to the point where he meets the woman of his dreams. In the romantic stage, the outlook is promising. Here is a woman (at last) who appears to accept him for who he is. She honors his specialness as he honors hers. Nothing stays the same, however, and changes occur as the relationship develops.

The longer he is with his partner, the more his unconscious feelings about the feminine have an impact on the way he relates to her. In most cases, he can sense that things are beginning to go awry but he is not really in touch with these feelings and thus not in touch with his own responsibility for the breakdown. He is unaware that he is in a protected stance with her. Furthermore, nothing has occurred in his life to alter the covenant he made with his mother. His rational mind compensates (as it always has) by doing its best to build a case against his partner. This means, of course, it must be her fault!

On top of all this, as the new relationship progresses, his partner expresses a need for more intimacy, for a deeper connection below the (unconscious and unrecognized) masks they are both hiding behind. She wants to talk about things. She begins to press him to bring out his feelings. But he doesn't know what his feelings are! He just knows what he thinks. He can't figure out what she is getting at. The only thing he can see is that his partner is becoming more demanding and less accepting, wanting him to be something he isn't (or doesn't know how to be). His psyche begins to sense "mother" closing in on him again. The only way he knows how to deal with this dilemma is to withdraw emotionally and rationalize even more—after all, such a strategy worked before.

Unconsciously, he increasingly "sees" his wife as his mother and begins to react to her the same way he did with his actual mother. If he was a good boy for his mother, he becomes a good boy with his partner. If he was withdrawn, defiant, or defensive with his mother, he becomes the same with his partner.

When he starts behaving this way, his partner feels angry and rejected. First off, she hates the prospect of being related to as his mother; she wants to be related to as a woman in her own right. She increasingly senses that he is not in touch with himself, and a man not genuinely in touch with himself has little to offer in terms of sustaining intimate nourishment. On top of all this, she can't quite get over the feeling that he is still attached to his mother (more than he is to her). Over time she feels hungrier and demands more. Guess what he does.

At the same time all of this is going on, he "remembers" the training from his mother, which taught him that he ought to be seen as the most special of special by women. He ought to be waited on hand and foot. He is supposed to be able to heal women by providing a meaning for their existence! However, as time goes by, his wife is less and less willing to let him define her and he can't figure out why she is fighting him. She seemed to be so willing to surrender to him during the romantic phase!

All this could be quite amusing if one were to stand back and view it objectively. Unfortunately, however, the outcome is generally not funny, as the overbonded mother has essentially taught her son to be a baby forever. In reaction to his mother, the overbonded son closes off his feelings and loses consciousness of a large part of who he is. As we have seen repeatedly, a man who is closed off emotionally and uncon- scious of the fact is clearly going to be handicapped when the time comes to enter into an intimate relationship of his own.

Overbonded sons might be skilled at seducing woman during the initial stages of relationship but they are not capable of supplying the substantial emotional support that will be required to keep intimacy fulfilling and juicy over the long term. His woman eventually ends up feeling isolated, unsupported, and emotionally undernourished. She doesn't feed him in return and he feels increasingly distanced and alone. At this point, the wife of this grown, overbonded man gets pregnant and this time it's a girl!

A Female Child Arrives to Bonded Parents

Now, let's take this same father, who has begun by now to withdraw from his partner. He has begun to sense that his wife is too controlling and/or too weak and self-centered to give him the support from the feminine he really needs. His sex life has probably cooled considerably. He lives in his head and tells himself everything is "fine." Underneath, although he is probably unwilling to acknowledge it to himself, he is wounded emotionally. He was already wounded when he came into the relationship and a number of experiences since the marriage have wounded him further, making him even more reluctant to open his vulnerable areas to his wife. He might play out the role of a strong man, but underneath he feels quite alone. And now he has a daughter!

With the arrival of a daughter, many forces and instinctual patterns are set into play and, in some ways, the drama is even more complicated than that of mother and son. One of the complications is that he, like many men, may be so wounded (though unconscious of his wounding) that he will abandon his daughter. Being emotionally immature and out of touch with himself, he is overwhelmed by the prospect of fathering. Rather than feel any of this, he seals himself off emotionally and unknowingly deprives his daughter of what she most needs from him— his authentic masculine presence.

Especially immature types depart physically and head for some less stressful pasture. Infantile at heart, they are totally unable to rise to the challenge of being anything for anybody. Men who stay physically present *but depart emotionally* might "think" they are doing the right thing, and will have great difficulty understanding why, years later, their daughters have dysfunctional relationships with men and come back at them with accusations of neglect.

A father in a bonded relationship enters into a silent pact with his daughter. Unconsciously, he says something like, "I'm not getting what I need from your mother and I want you to bring me the tenderness I am missing. I am not being accepted by your mother but I want *you* to accept me for who I am. In return, I'll see you as special, far more special than your mother. I'll support you as much as I am able. Let's join forces and have a special relationship that will exclude all others."

For some daughters it's a hard deal to pass up. These daughters unconsciously respond with something like: "No problem, Dad. I can feel you are wounded. I'll mother you and care for you better than Mom does. I'll accept you. Just adore me and I'll do anything. I know you carry this ideal in your mind—and I'll try to live up to it by doing everything *perfectly*." The silent pact is so strong that his daughter, in her adult years, will have a difficult time finding a man to take the place of her father.

Another group of daughters comes through with the opposite response. Their unconscious reply goes something like: "No deal. This is too much for me. I can feel I'm not being seen or accepted for who I am. I'll put on a mask; I'll rebel against you and, deep down, I'll create an ideal world in my mind where I won't be so hurt." If she allows herself to feel at all, in her adult years she will frequently find herself feeling disappointed by and rageful toward the flesh-and-blood men who do come into her world.

Once again, on the surface, the special bond this father has with his daughter looks ideal, especially in the early years. He appears to be doing his job very competently. He thinks well of himself and is admired by others for being a good father. The good mother, in the meantime, overrides her deeper feelings about losing her husband's heart and may even tell herself she is happy that her daughter is getting so much love and attention. The marriage may be unfulfilling but "at least, he is a good father."

Once again, let's fast-forward to puberty. This is often a time when the overbonding between father and daughter starts to become uncomfortable. Sexuality is present but nobody wants to feel it. The major tendency for the father is to begin to withdraw emotionally from her. Sexual feelings at this time are too much for the daughter to handle and she also withdraws in one way or another. Some daughters close off their sexuality and become "good girls," some rebel and become bad girls, some counterattack, some refuse to budge, and some flee the family altogether. Whatever may be the outer behavior, both father and daughter end up feeling abandoned and isolated. There is much anger under the surface.

The daughter comes into adulthood with lots of repercussions from this overbonding. Her relationship with her father has taught her that the way to be with men is to mother them. She got the message that her sexuality is dangerous and, despite their appearing to be powerful, men are really not able to handle it. She has learned of a special, idealized feminine—a feminine of the mind, a feminine of perfection—toward which she must strive if she is to be accepted by men.

Beneath the mask, all bonded daughters feel defiant and determined to preserve some sense of self, especially against the masculine. They also feel very special and/or in need of adoration by men. So as she feels insecure because she has never been unconditionally accepted just for being who she is, deep down she also feels enraged that she needs to behave in a certain way to be accepted by men. The good girl in her feels trapped, because good girls don't express anger. The bad girl also feels trapped, because even though she might rebel, she ends up feeling abandoned.

Let's fast-forward once again to the point where she meets her prince! Once again the romantic stage shows promise. Here is a man who seems, at last, to accept her for who she is. She honors his specialness as he honors hers. After a while, though, she begins to feel the same message coming through to her: just like her father, her husband wants the mothering he never really got. With her father she wasn't conscious of what it cost her, but now it's much clearer. She feels used. From her father, she at least got adoration and attention, but her husband is doing less and less of that. She wants something back for being the "mother." He ought to be adoring her and seeing her as precious and special, as her father did. Instead, she feels as if he just keeps on sucking off her more and more.

She resents getting so little in return for her mothering. Her sense of unfulfillment as a woman becomes increasingly apparent as time goes by. The more she knows of him, the more she sees he is incapable of supporting her in the way she feels she needs. Yet, the idea of being alone or rejected is terrifying to her little girl inside. She reaches the point where she doesn't believe she will ever be able to reach her fullest experience as a woman with him. Maybe . . . a child will do it for her.

Along comes a baby boy!

Please backtrack to the beginning of this section to see what happens with her and that baby boy. Clearly, the pattern has come full circle, ready to repeat itself once again. We can see that, in spite of their best intentions to do otherwise, parents who are dysfunctional in intimacy pass along dysfunction to their children. Parents caught in bonding patterns raise children who, if they are able to enter into intimate relationship at all, are doomed to recreate bonding patterns in their adult years.

OVERBONDING IS SEXUAL ABUSE

In the early days of our practice, Naomi and I were shocked by the number of clients who came through our door with sexual abuse issues. A few presented full-blown memories of such abuse, but the majority had only vague recollections that wouldn't go away. They felt as though something powerfully abusive had happened in their childhood and their instincts pointed toward their relationship with the opposite-sex parent.

It was especially confusing to them because this parent often didn't seem to fit the profile of an abuser and, if confronted directly, denied behaving abusively. However, that didn't usually quell the misgivings of these individuals, who wanted help "reconnecting" with the lost feelings so they could, at least, gain more understanding about why they were the way they were.

At first, we told ourselves, "Sexual abuse is a very big issue these days and we're just getting our share of clients who are confronting it." (It also caused us to wonder about what had really been going on in all those idyllic households during the 1940s and 1950s.) Then a shift in our thinking occurred about the time we came across another of John Bradshaw's gems. He says, "Sexual abuse occurs whenever the bond between parent and child is stronger than the bond between the parents themselves." In other words, *overbonding is a type of sexual abuse.*

We began to speculate that the reason we were seeing so many people trying to uncover sexual abuse issues from their past was that many of these individuals were suffering from the impact of overbonding. We also began to see that children who came from overbonded situations experienced many of the same repercussions in their adult years as children who were overtly sexually abused. This, in turn, led us to understand that overbonded children could learn a lot about their buried problems and concerns by studying cases where the sexual abuse had been acted out.

For example, children who are sexually abused typically come out of the experience with a deep-seated feeling of unworthiness and self-loathing. Underneath whatever mask is assembled in the journey toward adulthood, they hold very mixed feelings about the opposite sex—a prominent one being an abiding mistrust. Relaxing into their deepest sexual vulnerability is a lifelong challenge. They often end up with the vague but potent sense that somehow they are "victims" of the opposite sex and, in extreme cases, powerless in the face of everything that goes on around them. This feeling of inferiority, mixed with anger and mistrust, is evident to anyone who looks past the surface appearances, and it can be recognized as huge defiance, a determination to preserve some sense of self in what seems to be a very unsafe world.

People who, as children, were severely sexually abused might resent our including sexual abuse and overbonding in the same category—and they have a right to feel indignation. But they have the significant advantage of knowing they were abused. The severely abused child had a parent who clearly crossed the line between demonstrating love and using a child to fulfill personal needs. From this place of knowing (that is, of having those painful memories consciously available), the sexually abused child at least has the option of seeking help, and he or she knows what needs to be healed.

Overbonded children are often totally in the dark as to the reasons why they have difficulty with intimacy in their adult years. They are totally in the dark as to how defiant they are underneath their masks. They had a parent who, most likely, genuinely loved them *and*, looking at the shadow side of things, abused them. No clear boundary was transgressed. No conscious intent to abuse was present. To make it even more confusing, overbonded children, as adults, often *selectively* remember only the genuine love of their parent and even have a tendency to idealize that parent for being so "loving." They feel obligated to the parent. The effects of their being used or consumed remain dormant until difficulties with intimacy emerge in their adult years.

Awakening to the impact of overbonding with a child is not likely until an individual is willing to take an honest look at the impact of overbonding by his or her own parents. This is a difficult shadow-part to uncover and the tendency will be to pass it over in favor of letting bygones be bygones. After all, some of the feelings underneath it all are ugly and uncomfortable, and most people would rather focus on the lighter side of things.

The problem is that individuals who refuse to examine these feelings will almost inevitably recreate the same drama with their own children. If awakening to the impact of being overbonded by a parent is challenging, awakening to the impact created by overbonding with one's own child is almost impossible. Yet, such an awakening is what must occur if this widespread ailment is to be healed. Naomi and I feel the point must be made that overbonding is much more than an innocent neurosis acted out by a few misguided but well-intended individuals. In our view, parents who overbond with their children are victimizing them and contributing to what could be an extended legacy of dysfunction in adult intimacy.

The issue of parent-as-victimizer is a particularly difficult problem to address because parents who are most guilty of overbonding are the ones who are least conscious of who they are and what they really feel. They are, first, almost certainly out of touch with how undernourished they are in their adult relationship. And though they may *think* they are doing their very best at what they *think* is the right behavior, they are out of touch with the degree to which they need their children to provide them with an identity, a sense of meaning. They are out of touch with how much they need their children to provide the love they are not getting from their partner (and to make up for love they didn't receive themselves as children).

The dysfunctional relationship with their children often remains hidden from sight until the point arrives when the marriage finally collapses. At this point the charade breaks open and partners make a mad dash for the kids. They tell themselves they have the best interests of the children at heart, but there is, of course, a shadow side to this. In a bonded situation, the parents actually need the children more than the children need the parents. In the typical custody battle, parents are demonstrating their desperate need for the children (a need that has been there all along but is now being smoked out). The parents are also looking for a way of thwarting each other's desires; he wants to punish her for being so unloving to him; she wants to punish him for being so unloving to her. Unfortunately, in these all-out campaigns, both partners get so caught up in blaming the other that they will, once again, be unconscious of how *both* of them are using (and abusing) the children, making them pawns in their unconscious individual dramas. Once again, they fail to look inward, toward the real root of the difficulties.

Healthy Bonding and Overbonding: How to Tell the Difference

To be clear, the difference between healthy bonding and overbonding can involve one of those exquisitely fine lines which no parent is able to tread perfectly. A certain amount of overbonding at particular stages is probably inevitable. But leaving the matter there—at a mere acknowledgement of the potential for ambiguity—is not sufficient. The repercussions are too significant to ignore.

One of the reasons overbonding is so pervasive and difficult to deal with is that the behavior associated with healthy bonding is often indistinguishable from the behavior associated with overbonding. Overbonding parents may be "doing" all the right things; what creates the problem is their lack of awareness. Overbonding parents fail to grasp that the issue is not *what* they do so much as *why* they do it. In other words, the actual behavior is much less important than the "presence" and awareness of the parents. But in order to be present and aware, parents need to know who they are, and parents who are emotionally underdeveloped, who hide from their own shadow, are not able to be present and aware because they do not know themselves as fully as they "think" they do, if they think about it at all.

How can one recognize overbonding? Overbonding occurs when parents look for a child to make up for intimacy they lack in their own lives. It follows that the parents need principally to take a long, hard look at the relationship they have with each other. Are they getting their most important needs met *by each other*? How open are they to each other? Do they focus on the children as a way of avoiding each other? Are they expressing genuine love toward the children or are they over-involved and over-protecting? Are they acting out of mature mother/father or are they playing out mother/father *roles*? Do they want to have their children in the marital bed, to be unconscious buffers between them?

How much control is in the hands of the children and how much are they expected to be peers, or even the "parents" in the family? (Children are regularly portrayed that way in many television sitcoms, where oafish mothers and fathers are shown as subordinate to precocious kids.) The chances are that overbonding is present when parents look toward children to be their friends or advisors. Overbonding is present when a parent is not able to hold firm in the face of disapproval from the child. Overbonding is present when the child is not allowed to experience his or her own feelings, even if those feelings are painful. Parents who make the children into the center of their focus and totally organize their lives around the children are overbonding. And parents who can't talk about anything but the children are overbonding.

A "spousified" child—one who is expected to make up for the absence of a parent—is almost always overbonded with the parent who remains and is very likely to pass along the legacy of dysfunction in his or her future attempts at intimacy.

What Can Be Done?

Overbonding is one of those dynamics that is relatively easy to see in someone else's family. It is even relatively easy to see when one's spouse is overbonded. But it is very difficult to see when one is doing it oneself. In order to begin to remedy the situation, the partner who is excluded from the overbonding needs to speak up. That partner needs to be willing to express his or her feelings and demand more from the partner who is getting too caught up in the child. The overbonded parent will likely resent these demands at first, but the chances are that he or she also *wants* to be dragged away from the children. Perhaps the overbonded parent can be reminded that unless the spousal relationship can be strengthened, the children are going to pay a heavy price later on in their intimate relationships.

Unfortunately, all too many couples seem ready to endure a starved existence within a resigned relationship rather than do the work required to become more aware of themselves and their feelings. Many people much prefer to continue paying more attention to their children than to their partner. The price the child pays for this lazy approach doesn't become clear until many years later, when news of that child's first divorce arrives.

There Is Hope

Couples who are willing to look at themselves and find ways to get nourishment from their own relationship can effect remarkable changes in their family situation. However, overbonding is a part of the human drama that can never be eliminated. Continuous attention and determination to go inward to get one's needs met in constructive, conscious ways are required. As Naomi and I see things, people use addictions to avoid their inner feelings, and overbonding with the children is, very simply, an addiction . . . and a truly potent one, at that!

CONCLUDING REMARKS

In this chapter we were only able to hint at the enormity of a very large, complex problem. We focused primarily on the issue of overbonding. In order not to get lost in the complexity, we didn't spend much time on the children who were abused (or, at least, felt they had been abused) by being neglected or rejected by their opposite-sex parent early in life. However, one of life's fascinating ironies is that too little of something often creates the same effect as too much of it. Thus, in the realm of child rearing, we have seen that the parent who, for whatever reason, pays too little attention to a child may create the same effect as the parent who pays too much attention.

In other words, children who were abandoned by or received too little attention from their opposite-sex parent come through the experience with many of the same underlying feelings the overbonded child has. This neglected child also has a strong tendency to overbond with his or her own children—presumably as a way of compensating for *lack* of attention and love in his or her own life. People in one generation believe they will "solve" the effects of bonding patterns by doing the opposite of what *their* parents did, only to discover that they recreate the same effects with their own children through their lack of consciousness about themselves and what they are doing.

In this chapter, we didn't say anything about birth order, same-sex bondings, adoptions, or variations due to the age or developmental stage of parents, etc. We didn't talk about how overbonded children get alienated from their own gender and ultimately their own identity. The issue of sexual abuse and overbonding deserves a much more in-depth exploration but that material will have to wait for another book. At this point we are just trying to draw attention to the problem. Our hope is that bonded couples who truly want to do the best for their children will be able to recognize some parts of themselves in this chapter and be inspired to take a closer look at themselves.

Coming Up:

Naomi and I have seen that partners who are nourished by each other, sexually fulfilled by each other, and able to deal constructively with their anger have a much greater capacity to find the balance between nourishing their children and allowing the children the space to be themselves. In the next two chapters we will be exploring sexuality and anger in more detail.

10

SEX—WHO'S IN BED?

Just for one moment, let's ignore what our addictive, emotionally young, image- and power-oriented society has done with sex and get down to the basics of sexuality between two committed partners.

The essentials are these: sexual intimacy and touch are primary ways for partners to nourish and heal each other. Sexual relating is a type of emotional food. Sex helps us get out of our head and into our body, out of the perfection of our mind and into the raw power of our instinctual, feeling self. Regular sex and touching help us heal the small hurts and tensions we all experience in our daily lives (which, left unattended, could lead to bigger problems). Through giving and receiving physical pleasure in a committed relationship, partners can honor themselves in a way that is exclusive of all others. In short, regular sex and touch are a vital practice for healing the partners as individuals and for strengthening the bond of their relationship.

Why, then, do many couples have such a strong tendency to drift farther away from sexual intimacy and touch as their relationship progresses? Why is such an essential part of relationship, a part beneficial to both parties, so inclined to breakdown? Why do partners close off their vulnerable aspects to each other? Why do so many relationships evolve into a brother-sister or best-friends situation rather than one which heightens the adult masculine and feminine in both partners?

In this chapter, we will explore what happens when a man and women "forget" who they are as adults and bring their inner, immature boy and girl into the bedroom. For the purposes of our discussion, we will assume that the two individuals have ordinary sexual drives and basic human needs for intimacy. We will assume they are committed to each other and have a sincere desire to make their relationship work over the long term. We will *not*, though it is a common enough occurrence, deal with the obsessive use of sex to bolster a sense of personal power and/or to cover up intense feelings of unworthiness, as such an exploration is beyond the scope of this book.

Sexual Difficulties in Intimate Relationship

When things aren't going as well as they might sexually, both partners experience dismay and confusion. In earlier stages, their sex life was often passionate and alive (though extremely bonded couples may not have had mutually fulfilling sex even at the beginning). Now, however, it is sporadic at best and neither partner can really understand how it got to be that way. Frequently, one of them will have the puzzling recognition that this decline first became noticeable after their marriage or some other significant evidence of their commitment to the relationship.

Though one partner may be more vocal than the other, both have some reluctance about venturing any deeper into the issue. Long-standing sexual inhibitions may be present in one or both partners. Or if such inhibitions are not present, we can at least be sure that touchy, delicate egos are at stake. Both partners have some feelings of inadequacy and neither wants to expose any more vulnerability or accept any more responsibility than necessary. Most likely, neither wants to admit being needy. Partners may have a sense of what they want the other to do in bed but have difficulty expressing it directly.

When their sexual experience with one another has been deteriorating for any length of time, the couple has probably been through a number of conflicts over it and, as a result, has become tentative or outright defensive around the issue. Partners are frequently hyper-alert either to criticizing or to being criticized. They find that clear, honest communication without blame is difficult.

How can a couple progress from this point? Human sexuality is a complex issue and difficulties with it can be explored in many different ways. One therapeutic approach views sexual dysfunction as a technical problem to be solved. Presumably, an "answer" can be found by applying the correct techniques or through adjustments of behavior and/or attitude. Often the focus is placed on one partner more than the other. Sometimes this problem-solving approach helps, particularly at the earlier stages of relationship, but many times sexual dysfunction will re-emerge in a different form later on if the partners have not explored (or have refused to explore) the deeper, internal aspects of their situation.

Partners who want to explore their sexual difficulties as a communications issue might start to unravel the points of dissension by expressing some of their conflicting wants and needs around sexuality. Typically, conflicts exist about frequency and about differences in personal wishes regarding how they will engage in sex. For example, one partner wants sex more often than the other. Perhaps he wants her to initiate more. Or she wants more romancing outside the bedroom. He wants more oral sex. She wants more touching and time to warm up. One pushes for greater variety or more adventuresome sex and the other resists . . . and so on. Incidentally, though we have used specific genders here according to the usual stereotypes, these stances are not necessarily gender-specific. We have heard each of these demands from both genders. Further, at different times, the roles can reverse within the same relationship.

Whatever approach is taken, the obvious overall way to restore harmony when two individuals have conflicting needs is to seek out avenues of reconciliation and compromise. Presumably, after bringing their needs out into the open, both partners will be able to negotiate with each other and get their most important needs met, at least some of the time.

The sad reality, however, is that all too often sexuality *still* breaks down after this type of mediation. A period of time passes, after which one or both partners demonstrate a type of selective memory loss and "forget" about their part in the compromise. That partner may also "forget" over and over again! Often, if one partner is not rejecting, the other is. Apparently *one* of them needs to do the rejecting until something comes clear between them, though neither partner knows exactly what that mysterious "something" is.

Naomi and I have learned that when a couple has sexual difficulties, both partners are angry, so that's a clue. But why are they so angry? We know it's more than faulty technique or a failure of communication. We know the partners don't really *want* to compromise. Something must be going on here that is beneath the awareness of, and therefore hidden from, both individuals.

Both Partners Are Emotional Children (and Don't Want to Know It)

In previous chapters, Naomi and I emphasized that emotional immaturity frequently exists beneath the adult masks of intimate partners. We have also found that a lot can be learned about sexual difficulties when this shadow side is recognized and acknowledged. Understanding why two healthy, committed adults would starve themselves sexually is difficult, but seeing how two egocentric, needy, defended, emotionally young individuals have difficulty with lasting love is not difficult! Finally, we come to a viable answer to our questions. Let's take a closer look at how the inner emotional child affects sexual relating.

The Partners Are Egocentric

The egocentric, emotionally immature child has a worldview that revolves completely around self. When adult partners in a relationship remove their masks, they often discover they have not progressed very far from this way of looking at life! As we have seen, at the beginning of their relationship, they were probably able to disguise this self-involved child from their partner. Perhaps they were able to bring forth the playful, less inhibited, childlike parts of themselves. Each partner was probably taking care to put his or her best foot forward. However, we can be virtually assured that at the point they became more committed, their egocentric aspects started to peek through.

The egocentric child in each partner, in being so self-oriented, is not able to understand that the other partner is actually a different person. The egocentric child is so busy justifying its own view of things that the partner is essentially ignored. The egocentric child can't really understand conflicting needs because it automatically assumes its own needs come first and everybody else's needs are secondary.

The egocentric woman holds the view that her partner ought to be like her. With that reasoning, she assumes feelings *must* come first, before sexual openness, and that's just the way things ought to be. If he doesn't understand this, he must be defective. The emotional woman-child needs to have everything *her* way. To give him what he wants would cause her to feel as though she were being used. After a period of time, when she doesn't get her way, she gets angry and begins to withhold—just like a frustrated, egocentric child.

Similarly, the egocentric man maintains the view that his partner ought to be like him. She ought to be available and open to sex whenever he is ready. If she isn't ready when he is, she must be cold and rejecting. As his immature child sees it, doing it her way is akin to being controlled and dominated by her. After trying to initiate sex for a while and not getting what he wants, he just stops. Rather than expressing his feelings (hurt, angry, rejected, hopeless, etc.) he too begins to withhold, just like a frustrated, egocentric child.

This problem is compounded because the egocentric child has an expectation that its needs ought to be met without its even having to ask. The partner should automatically know what this child wants! In the child's view, a partner who isn't able to divine, to intuit, or otherwise to discern his or her sexual needs through mind-reading must not be loving. Furthermore, extremely egocentric children don't even know how to ask. They just expect their needs to be met and are perplexed when that doesn't happen.

Each Partner Expects a "Good Parent" in Bed

Once again, we see the immature emotional child with an implicit expectation that the partner ought to act more like an ideal parent than an adult man or woman. Thus a man-child silently expects his partner to accept him as unconditionally as an ideal mother would. She should nurture him and be present to meet his sexual needs. She shouldn't be angry or have any expectations of him. When he is not treated this way, he feels disappointed and starts to become quieter, to sulk like a child. The problem for him is that the more he withdraws, the angrier and more controlling she becomes. Instead of being a good mother, she increasingly acts out the bad mother.

He doesn't recognize his own emotional child, who is secretly demanding that ideal mother. He won't allow himself to become aware of how small he feels in relation to an angry, controlling mother. His response to the whole situation is to tell himself he needs more "space." In other words, his egocentric child part wants things his way and at his pace. When his partner shows fewer signs of going along with this and increases her attempts at control, he begins to withhold his affection and sexuality. (A man who is extremely young emotionally might find that withholding his sexual energy is the only control he can exert against his powerful, controlling mother.)

On the other side of this equation, an emotionally young woman has a secret expectation that her partner will give her as much attention as an ideal father would. He should be totally supportive and unconditionally accepting. He should be sensitive to her feelings and give her exactly what she wants. He shouldn't be angry or have any expectations. When he doesn't treat her this way, she is disappointed and ultimately gets angry and resentful. She withdraws and/or becomes more demand-ing.

As time goes by in the relationship, the emotional woman-child within her begins to realize she doesn't have the good father she was expecting. In fact, she increasingly recognizes she is with an egocentric child, and that he can't possibly give her the amount of attention she desires. As she demands more, he gets "smaller" and retreats farther into himself. Even if he does attempt to fulfill her needs, the expectations of her emotional child are so great that he couldn't possibly succeed, and she starts to feel hopeless. She feels a lack of trust in him—he can't be depended on to be the good father. In her disappointment and hopeless-ness, she begins to withhold sexually.

The Partners Blame Each Other

At the beginning of a relationship the inner "children" feel excited and hopeful about the prospect of being with their new partner. Both have an implicit expectation of *receiving* a steady flow of unconditional love (similar to what a good parent would give) but neither is capable of *delivering* it for extended periods. The egocentric child expects everything to come its way without having to give anything in return and is shocked to discover that the partner doesn't automatically follow through with unconditional love (and actually places conditions on what love *is* there). As time goes by, these same children begin to feel hopeless about the relationship and undernourished by it, without really understanding why.

When this hidden child feels thwarted in having its essential needs met (as will inevitably happen over the course of the relationship), it has to find some way to justify the indignity of the situation. Rather than undertake an internal self-examination (and the egocentric child doesn't really even know how to look inward), the partners have a tendency to deny the existence of the emotional child within and increasingly to create scenarios in their own minds that shift the blame onto the partner. He focuses on her as the problem and judges her for her faults. *She*

163

should change. She sees him as the problem and rejects him. *He should change.* Blaming and self-justification build, and on it all goes until they're lucky to have sex once every couple of weeks!

(These inner dynamics are also prominent in immature child types who can't find their way into fulfilling relationship to start with. Rather than look inward for ways to understand their inability to attract a satisfactory mate, they tell themselves there just aren't any responsible, mature, loving, available members of the opposite sex available. Eventually they decide it is better to be alone and not have to be so compromised by those children types "out there.")

Emotionally immature individuals essentially set themselves up as victims. They see their lack of love and fulfilling sex as their partner's fault. Yet their internal child is much more than a victim of circumstances. This child plays a very active role in the power struggle that invariably emerges when two partners feel they aren't getting their sexual needs met in the relationship.

The Partners Struggle for Power and Control

When I recall periods of sexual drought in my first marriage, I remember secretly resolving that *I* wasn't going to be the first to initiate sex! Why should *I* always be the one who risked being rejected? I had initiated sex the past "x" number of times and now it was her turn. Even if months had to go by without our having sex, I'd rather starve than back down from this resolve. I wasn't going to expose my need and I wasn't going to be vulnerable—at least, not first.

Though I was not aware of it at the time, this was the voice of my immature child. In the arena of sexuality and power struggles, the unspoken underlying statements of this internal child often go something like this: She says, "I will open to receive you sexually *after* you listen to me and attend to me." He says something like, "I will listen to you and attend to you *after* you open to receive me sexually." Though it is seldom stated out loud, the clear implication is, "I want what I want before you get what you want" or "I won't appreciate you until you appreciate me" or "You have to accept me before I'll accept you."

These immature inner children are very stubborn and defiant. One partner says he or she can stay closed and do without sex and intimacy *longer* than the other can. One insists that the other is *more* at fault. On it goes, with each partner waiting for the other to make the *first* move, the *first* show of vulnerability. Who is going to be *first* to admit to neediness? Until some consciousness is brought to the underlying struggle for control and power, the chances are that neither partner will make the first move. Both will avoid anything that might be construed as weakness.

On the surface, both partners simply feel wronged and have a long list of justifications to support their view that the other one should surrender first and/or make the first move. Underneath the surface, we have something akin to the three-year-olds we talked about earlier who were in a sandbox fighting over the pail and shovel. Each partner is getting angrier at the unwillingness of the other to surrender first. And an angry, stubborn child can be unmovable!

From this point on, a downward spiral begins. These emotional "children" will punish each other even if their own sex life must be sacrificed! Neither partner is willing to back down. Both get more frustrated (which is another way of saying "angrier"). They spend less and less time with one another. Too much attention and affection get directed toward the kids. The power struggle extends to other areas of the couple's life, and more difficulties emerge. Anger builds. Blaming continues. Both partners, as usual, are unwilling to acknowledge how emotionally young they feel underneath the struggle. At the point where a willingness to expose vulnerability to each other is most needed, they become the most defensive.

The times these partners do come together sexually turn out to be less and less rewarding. Because of all the business below the surface, they are over-reactive to each other. Both are hyper-alert to any sign of rejection. Neither wants to experience any loss of power relative to the other. Tensions are high and partners have difficulty relaxing. With longer periods between sex, the male has to fight against ejaculating quickly. The female has difficulty orgasming. When sex is awkward, tense, and short-lived, a couple has less desire to try it again. Partners increasingly seek rewards outside their relationship.

As their sex life slows or stops altogether, partners don't feel nourished. When sexual needs are not being met, anger follows, and if that anger is not expressed, it accumulates. Defenses strengthen, vulnerability diminishes, criticism increases. As the partners become increasingly rigid and defended, less opportunity is present for personal growth or movement. Couples withdraw from each other and/or start experiencing the quiet contempt that one so often sees in "experienced" couples who have dropped into resignation with each other.

SEX IS NOT FOR CHILDREN

Bringing egocentric children into the bedroom is clearly not going to lead to a satisfying sexual life. An emotionally young woman who is still living out a daughter role and dealing with men-as-father is out of touch with her own needs and decisions in regard to sexuality. The daughter part of a woman often feels as if her duty is to have sex for *his* benefit rather than for her own. Because she believes she is doing it for him, she will inevitably feel used after a period of time. When she feels used, anger accumulates. Large amounts of accumulated, silent anger usually result in a closed vagina.

The immature woman who habitually adopts the mother role in relationship usually has difficulty letting go of control and, of course, this is carried into the bedroom as well. She silently blames her partner for being weak and inadequate. She also smolders with anger. The angry woman who has difficulty letting go of control and/or senses the need to act in a certain way for her partner's benefit will have difficulty orgasming regularly, if she experiences orgasm at all. She is often left feeling unsatisfied and frustrated after sex. After these types of experiences occur for a while, she will not be inclined to encourage more of them.

An emotionally young man who primarily acts out the boy type is not very fulfilling as a sexual partner over the long term (and maybe not even in the short term). Being something of a narcissist, he evaluates himself by the way his partner responds to him but isn't completely present in the fullness of the experience. When viewing himself as a healer/savior in the early stages of relationship he can be potent, but an emotionally young man who is still taking the women-as-mother perspective will eventually feel powerless in close quarters with women. Men in this situation, if they are able to achieve erection, have a very strong tendency to ejaculate quickly.

The emotionally young man who adopts the father role in relationship needs to choose powerless daughters or, at least, be assured that his power is acknowledged before sex is possible. These types can be great with affairs (or with women they pay) but not so great with committed partners. Whereas the son type has a tendency to ejaculate too quickly, the controlling father type might be so controlling that he eventually finds himself having difficulty ejaculating at all.

Two emotional children who refuse to become conscious of their inner nature and thus refuse to grow up authentically often find themselves in a brother-sister relationship after a few years. Both might have affection and caring for one another, but when "brother" and "sister" are in bed, it doesn't make for great sex.

Because they are both emotionally so young, child partners are terribly afraid of ending the relationship altogether. Though they may reject each other sexually, each is careful to inject just the minimum amount of juice into the relationship to keep the other from actually leaving. They just want to starve their partners, not finish them off!

When one partner doesn't do as the other wishes, emotionally young individuals have a tendency to want to punish their partner. Some punish subtly by withdrawing their enthusiasm and playing the martyr. Overt punishers become verbally or physically abusive. Passive punishers flirt

167

flagrantly or have affairs. When the desire to punish or prove oneself is present, mutually fulfilling, long-lasting sexuality is doomed.

WHAT CAN BE DONE
TO ENHANCE SEXUAL RELATING?

In Bed, Aware and Truthful Adults Need to Replace Immature Children

Let's face it. We all have a part within us that is extremely egocentric. All of us at one time or another want to be cared for by an ideal partner who is willing to act like a perfect parent. We all have an inner part that wants to have its needs met first. We all have a part that will fight to the end for control. We all have a part that is stubborn, defensive, and unwilling to become vulnerable.

In order to enhance their sexual relating, both partners in an intimate relationship must find ways to bring other, more mature aspects of themselves into their bed. As we have said many times already, awareness comes first. But in order for the partners to become aware, truth needs to be told. If they are aware and truthful, all the issues that come up can be dealt with. If they are unwilling to recognize truth, they invariably arrive at a stuck point. They end up carrying on (or attempting to carry on) in a fantasy relationship that never works out in reality.

The amusing part is that both partners already know the other is egocentric and has immature parts; each, upon hearing it out in the open, at least knows he or she is hearing something truthful. When partners are willing to acknowledge their *own* feelings of neediness, hurt, anger, fear of rejection, hunger for power, and so forth, they have a place from which to begin being with each other, rather than fighting each other. When couples are ready to express feelings and become vulnerable enough to reveal how much they need to be seen by their partners as attractive and acceptable, things can start to move forward. Sex is a body experience for adults. It just can't be maintained when two children are trying to live in a fantasy or delusion and won't speak the truth.

The Need for Surrender:
Would I Rather Be in Control or Have Good Sex?

We have already seen that the immature child part will not be the one who surrenders first (remember, its motto is "Deadness before Surrender"). And we have seen that sexual energy will not flow freely when struggles over power and control are underway. Where can we go from here?

Someone has to surrender. Though in actual practice they usually are not much better at it than men, women seem to feel more at ease with this concept. In fact, Naomi and I work with many women in their midlife and, almost in chorus, they say they want to be with a man to whom they can surrender sexually. But they don't want to surrender to a little boy and they don't want to surrender to an inflated father type; they want to surrender to a man who can hold them and meet them in their feelings. These women sense that letting go of control in this way is one of their primary avenues into the discovery of the mature feminine.

Men have difficulty even with the idea of it. Surrender is immediately equated with "giving up," which is equated with weakness and defeat. And the appearance of defeat is to be avoided at all costs. (Of course, it is the insecure, egocentric little-boy part who is most worried about image and bolstering a sense of power.)

Men have an easier time when the word "allow" is substituted for surrender. Thus: a man needs to learn to "allow" both himself and his partner to be authentic. In order to "allow" fully, he has to let go of "doing." He must let go of posturing, proving, judging, defending. He must let go of his desire to hold himself above it all. In short the *acceptance* he is looking for from his intimate partner is exactly the quality he needs to embody himself.

The state of surrender (as opposed to the "doing" of surrender) is very different from giving up or being defeated in some way. Far from being a loss of self, it can be a finding of self, the self that exists behind the mask. When a person begins the process of surrender, he or she opens the door to the deeper truth of being and ultimately a more authentic, richer experience of power than that which comes from posturing. When couples can share this form of power, sexuality is enriched and becomes very reinforcing. When sex is reinforcing in this way, one becomes much more determined not to let it fall away.

Essentially, coming to terms with surrender means coming to terms with powerlessness. When two individuals can come to terms with both power *and* powerlessness, the sexual energy between them has a chance of continually expanding. The power a person can generate through knowing and being accepting of his or her powerlessness far surpasses the delusionary state that exists when two emotionally young individuals are trying to prove to each other that they are powerful—when, in fact, they are anything but.

These concepts about surrender may seem sensible enough in theory, but our teaching and our personal experiences indicate that really taking them in is hard, and implementing them is even harder. A person who has spent a lifetime "in control" has great difficulty even conceptualizing another way of living. Letting go of control is associated with chaos, weakness, failure, and defeat. Letting go of control, which requires a willingness to jump into the abyss and experience vulnerability in front of one's partner, is the last thing people want to do when they are confronting years of stored resentment and habitual defensive stances with each other. It requires overcoming a lifetime of patterning, of upholding images of the self.

Another way of putting this is that the immature inner child only wants to feel safe. It is not willing to put itself in a position where it might have to risk vulnerability; it is not willing to surrender. To the child, surrender means giving up, and the egocentric child will do almost anything to avoid the appearance of losing. Only the adult man or woman has enough internal strength to be able to experience surrender and feel comfortable.

Irony of the "No Surrender" Position in Relationship

We've seen that the emotionally young woman is looking for a "real man," but as soon as she commits, she begins to engage in a power struggle with him. She closes sexually or rejects him in some other way. He becomes undernourished. A man who is undernourished will have more difficulty developing the balanced, adult masculine power she is looking for. In other words, by sexually rejecting him, she helps to keep him being the little boy she doesn't really want.

The emotionally young man is looking for a "real woman," but as soon as he commits, he does everything he can to avoid his feelings of powerlessness and engages in a power struggle with her. He withdraws emotionally and refuses to nourish her in the ways she needs. She doesn't feel supported in developing her adult feminine power—the healing, juicy feminine he is instinctively looking for. By withdrawing into his own world, he thwarts the development of what he wants.

It's a dilemma. We "think" we want powerful partners and yet we often unconsciously act in ways that disempower them. Through our lack of consciousness, we actually create and sustain scenarios that keep us where we "think" we don't want to be. We keep ourselves stuck.

Once again: partners must develop more consciousness about their wholeness, about who they really are, if their relationship is going to function more smoothly. In the realm of sex, they must continually be asking themselves, "Who's in bed with us, anyway?"

NUTS & BOLTS OF SEXUAL RELATING

In this chapter we have focused on the importance of bringing emotionally immature aspects to consciousness, the importance of truth, and the importance of surrender. Aside from these lofty ideals, some very basic nuts-and-bolts issues need also to be addressed if a couple wants to maintain an active, mutually nourishing sex life.

Touch Is Essential

No amount of insight or understanding of deeper issues will be of any use in enhancing sexuality unless a couple is willing to give and receive touch on a regular basis. In the eight years Naomi and I have been together, I doubt that a dozen days have gone by during which we didn't touch each other at least ten minutes a day. I admit to being startled by the number of couples who report they cannot seem to find the time and/or energy for such a simple and fundamental expression of caring.

If a man only touches when he wants sex, his partner can't be faulted for feeling used and eventually withdrawing. If a woman refuses to initiate touch, his partner can't be faulted for withdrawing and eventually looking for other ways to nourish himself. Partners who touch only sparingly can't blame their partners for over-reacting or under-reacting upon being touched. The solution to this problem is simple, yet all too often it goes unheeded. Touch each other and do it a lot!

When given the homework of touching ten minutes each day, couples often treat this simple exercise as a revelation. As they incorporate this practice into their experience, it often serves to harmonize and enhance their relating—sexual and otherwise—for a time. Yet when we check a few weeks later, we find that almost every couple has dropped back into a pattern of not touching regularly. The reasons for stopping the practice are plentiful and a few might even be valid, but the truth is that a couple who can't find ten minutes a day for touch is almost certainly not really interested in sustaining a rewarding sex life together.

Like it or not, we live in a culture that encourages us to live in our heads—in our thoughts, in our minds—as opposed to our bodies. I can use myself as an example. As I spend increasing amounts of time at my computer—writing, thinking about, analyzing, and reflecting on what I have learned so I can report it clearly to others—I can get increasingly out of touch with my body. The more that happens, the more difficult a time I have getting back and making that body-connection again. I discover that being in my head is addictive, and I must make a deliberate, determined effort to return to my body (where I'll find my sexuality). I appreciate Naomi's ability to recognize when I am out of my body, and to invite me back in compassionately, creatively, and noninvasively. It's a valuable awareness/skill for a partner to develop, and she and I both recommend it to others.

Commitment Is Essential

When Naomi and I ask women what they need in order to experience their deeper sexuality, commitment is always first or second on the list. Whether a woman is conscious of it or not, when her partner is not committed, she feels as if he is on the lookout for someone else, usually "someone better." She feels as if he is saying she is not good enough for him (which, in fact, he *is* saying, implicitly). A woman who isn't regarded as good enough for a commitment by her partner is not going to open to vulnerability and sexuality at the deepest levels. A man who wants to have a sexually enthusiastic partner over the long term needs to commit.

Emotionally young men usually have more difficulty with commitment. The emotional boy inside feels he will lose control and power if he commits, so he maintains a sense of power by keeping one foot out the door, by holding part of himself aloof from his partner, with the secret expectation that "one day" the ideal sexual partner will appear. Until he comes to terms with commitment, deeper ongoing sexual intimacy with a flesh-and-blood partner is going to elude him.

We should note here that many couples have made a decision to stay in the relationship but haven't really made a *commitment* to each other. The distinction may appear to be subtle when it's expressed in words, but the difference it makes in day-to-day feelings and in sexual possibilities is significant.

Meat-and-Potatoes Sex

Our culture is oriented toward seeking the ideal, and it doesn't fail to do that in regard to sexuality. Even in this chapter we've made many references to *deeper, more intense* (thus ideal) levels of sex. While it's true that Naomi and I, like most couples, aim for the mystical experiences that are possible when a couple is in deep sexual communion, it is also true that we aren't able to sustain those levels of intensity without substantial periods of what we call "meat-and-potatoes sex" in between.

My guess is that the only people who can sustain a Tantric pitch are those who make a business of teaching it. The rest of us make a living doing something else! Daily schedules and family demands take a toll on our energies. Many times, sex must take on a lower priority.

As unromantic and unspontaneous as this may sound, when our schedules keep us unusually busy or preoccupied, Naomi and I often make appointments to have sex. The playful, idealistic child inside rebels at this and wants to keep sexuality active through magic. The reality of life in our culture is different, however. During holidays or breaks from work, the playful child can have its time. But during periods of busy schedules and outside obligations, sexuality has a tendency to fall away unless she and I make a determined effort to organize time for it. Both partners must take responsibility for this scheduling, rather than one of them waiting for the other and silently moving into blame when sexual intensity begins to diminish. When the timing isn't perfect and when bodies aren't at peak performance, it's time for meat-and-potatoes sex!

Increases in Pleasure Do Not Come through Technique

Emotionally young individuals often believe sexual pleasure is heightened by seeking out the ideal partner and developing the right techniques. In the earlier stages of life and relationship, this approach may have some validity. But then one is continually tempted to be seeking a new ideal partner or a different technique, since satisfaction always diminishes when the partner's less-than-ideal parts start to show through and a limit to what can be attained through the refinement of technique is approached.

Naomi's and my experience at this stage of our own midlife is that increasing pleasure is directly related to the capacity to surrender, to allow vulnerability. Contrary to the transitory effect of seeking the "ideal," the increase of pleasure that comes when both partners let go of control naturally leads to their desiring more sex. When partners begin to realize that increasing amounts of pleasure come through increasing amounts of vulnerability and truth—whereas pleasure decreases with seduction, masking, and defending—they are encouraged toward increased personal growth and awareness. When this process begins to take hold, partners cultivate a natural desire to nourish themselves and each other in whatever way is needed, as opposed to becoming locked into power struggles, in which both end up getting starved.

No Anger, No Sex

The emotional child within believes that when anger is expressed in relationship, sex goes out the window. The adult knows it is actually the opposite. From what Naomi and I have seen and experienced, partners who can't deal with anger have no hope of sustaining fulfilling sexuality. Couples who are having sexual difficulties and want to heal must be willing to explore anger—in themselves and in each other. That's what the next chapter is about.

11

THE WEAVE
OF ANGER AND INTIMACY

We are devoting a chapter to anger because, in our experience, partners who can't deal constructively with anger have little hope of developing deeper, enduring intimacy. Genuine intimacy requires two whole individuals, and feelings of anger—part of the experience of aliveness and passion—are an important aspect of what being human is all about. Contrary to what the emotionally immature inner child usually believes, the expression of anger can actually serve to enhance intimacy. But in order to use it constructively, one needs to face anger when it is present and develop skills in expressing and receiving it.

Anger in relationship is a big subject to tackle in just one chapter. We decided the most effective way to address it would be to develop a case example of a typical couple who have problems with anger, then follow it up with wide-ranging commentary to provide a more thorough understanding.

Once again, our intent is to spark some insights and new ways of looking at things. First, however, we want to be clear that we are not addressing the experience of pathological or psychopathic anger—where, for example, it is used to dominate, intimidate, or abuse by

177

impulsive, unstable, immature individuals. That is definitely beyond the scope of this discourse.

SOME BASICS:
HOW WE SEE ANGER AND ITS ROLE IN RELATIONSHIP

We are dealing here with a feeling which every person would probably define differently. From our point of view, anger is *a type of energy*, an energy given forth from the body. It is part of the repertoire of human feelings and is available all the time. Anger energy, much like sexual energy, is a form of raw power. It can be a vital resource but, in order to be really useful, needs to be harnessed and channeled (as opposed to swallowed). Like any other resource, anger can be misused.

The emotionally young individual is very afraid of the misuse of anger energy, viewing it as something to be controlled, expunged, transcended, or (at least) avoided. The emotionally young individual also tends to be disconnected from his or her own deeper feelings of anger. Naomi and I observe that people who do not deal with anger, or who confront it as an unwelcome adversary, tend to be handicapped in their personal expression of life. Why is this so?

Anger and personal will (or personal power, the ability to assert yourself effectively in the world) are closely interrelated. In fact, if you were able to trace these two experiences back into your body, you might discover that they originate in about the same place. Individuals who block their expression of anger also block their expression of personal will. And individuals who have difficulty exercising their personal will also experience difficulty when faced with the need to put themselves forward in the world. In short, people who have difficulty expressing anger seldom live up to their potential as adult men or women.

Soon enough, partners in intimate relationship realize that no two people can live in close proximity without conflict. They sometimes want different things. Boundaries get violated. A partner will be thoughtless, selfish, or act unjustly from time to time. Each partner needs to have anger available for those times when transgressions are perceived to have occurred, as a direct expression of anger is often the most efficient way to restore balance and harmony. When anger is not expressed, an illusion of harmony may be sustained a little longer, but the underlying situation gradually deteriorates. Couples who refuse to deal with anger invariably find themselves sinking deeper into a kind of interpersonal mire, as though they were swimming in peanut butter.

Expression of Anger in Relationship—What Do We Mean?

Anger is a personal feeling and comes from within. The *expression* of anger has to do with moving it from the inside to the outside. Some people say the expression of anger allows it to be "released." That may be so, however, it is not released in the sense of being sent off into the ether, never to be felt again (as the emotionally young might hope); anger is never eliminated once and for all, nor would that even be desirable. The expression of anger is simply a movement of energy. Anger that is expressed clears out and opens the self. Anger that is not expressed—i.e., that is held in or repressed—tends to clog up the self.

When anger is not held in, life and feelings continue to move to the next experience and the next, whatever they may be. Perhaps love or sadness or fear or joy or excitement. In other words, when anger is released appropriately, life moves along; life flows. When anger is held in, and especially when it is habitually held in, life becomes overcontrolled and stifled. Withheld anger also seems to beget more anger. The accumulation may take a long time and its results may not be obvious for a while, but anger that is not expressed will eventually have repercussions, whether we want it to or not. (Most people can picture an old relative who has many years of unexpressed anger carved into his or her face.)

Expressing anger is not as easy as it might sound, especially for individuals who have held their feelings back for an entire lifetime. Expressing anger is a skill that needs to be learned and refined just like any other skill. Individuals who have habitually repressed anger often need to go through the motions of acting it out before they can develop the ability to actually express it. Extremely blocked individuals may even be afraid to go through the motions of anger and they justify their unwillingness to do so by telling themselves they just aren't angry at that particular moment. They lie to themselves.

In our experience, anger is most effectively expressed through a combination of sound and movement. Anger energy can also be effectively expressed through the eyes. By watching and sensing a person's eyes, an observer can begin to differentiate between going through the motions of acting out anger and reaching the point where anger energy is truly present.

When we work on anger with couples, we allow no physical contact, though the people doing the expressing might want to do some old-fashioned pillow bashing or whatever they sense will help them move the anger out of their body. We encourage what we call "clean" expressions of anger. The cleanest expressions of anger are nonverbal, with only sound and eye contact. Many people believe they need to "express" their anger verbally, but as soon as the words are out, what usually becomes evident is that they are actually endeavoring to get the upper hand by blaming, attempting to prove themselves right, or trying to make the other person smaller in some way. These verbal displays are quite different from direct expressions of anger energy.

What Is _Not_ Expression of Anger?

This seems to be a strange question but because so much misconception exists about anger in relationship, we believe it is worth attempting to answer.

Anger is a _feeling_ and, by itself, has no connection with "doing." The expression of anger is different from the desire to control, punish, injure, or damage. The expression of anger is different from needing to prove oneself superior or dominant. The expression of anger is different from exacting revenge. And expressing anger is very different from _emitting_ anger—the process that occurs when a person is noticeably angry but refuses to acknowledge it openly.

180

Most of us implicitly equate the expression of anger with a need to produce a result. It is important to recognize that these are two distinct processes: (1) the expression of anger and (2) the need to take action. The expression of anger has to do with oneself only, whereas the need to take action is usually in reaction to that which is outside of self. Expressing anger is a personal experience; the desire to act it out has to do with justifying oneself, dominating, avoiding powerlessness, and so forth. As we shall see in our case example, expressing angry feelings actually requires vulnerability, whereas the need to have something happen is more about power and invulnerability.

For instance, in regard to the distinction between anger and aggression: expression of anger releases and relieves; aggression does not. Aggression is not the clean expression of a feeling; it's a "doing," an attack, and nothing is really released during aggression; the stakes just keep needing to go higher; ever-increasing amounts of damage are inflicted as aggressors, having a desperate need to prove themselves worthy, strive to bolster themselves. In our experience, aggression is most likely to come from those who are out of touch with themselves and refuse to locate and express their anger.

In short, anger is a feeling, and the expression of angry feelings is closely related to the expression of one's life juices. Expressing and receiving feelings of anger releases the self and enables one to be more alive, more emotionally nourished. Expressing and receiving anger ultimately allows one to be more available to feel love.

In intimate relationship, couples will engage in all manner of activities, both active and passive, to punish or dominate each other, but seldom is the clean expression of anger involved. Let's take a look at a typical couple who have come to counseling and are just beginning to learn about expressing anger.

CASE EXAMPLE: Allison & Dan

Seven years and two children into their relationship, Allison and Dan are not happy about the way things are going. Their passion has disappeared and they are in power struggles a lot of the time over small issues. On the surface, both appear to be controlled and contained, but it doesn't take an expert to see they are both filled with anger. In the first two minutes of our session with them, Naomi and I recognize they are both so defensive that a *lot* of words will be required before we even begin to crack through the surface of the shells they have built around themselves. We could move much faster into the core issues if Allison and Dan were willing to get to some actual feelings.

We spend a few minutes talking about anger and they both agree that they hold a lot of it within themselves. Both intellectually accept that getting some of this anger out would be good. Then, perhaps, they could move forward without so much defensiveness and control. She, being somewhat more in touch with her feelings, agrees to start.

The partner who first volunteers to express anger often begins with "you did . . . " or "you are . . . " statements, followed by a lengthy and detailed discourse on the partner's shortcomings. Allison starts in this typical fashion. We interrupt her and point out that she is not expressing anger. She's telling him who he is, scolding, attempting to prove herself superior and make him small; but she's not expressing angry feelings. (Essentially she is acting out of her "controlling mother," which will only result in more defensiveness from him.)

Allison starts up again, this time detailing resentments from the past. We interrupt her again and point out that this is not expression of anger, either. Recounting past events in front of an unbiased observer can be important for individuals who have a big stockpile of stored grievances, but in doing so they are essentially assuming the elevated role of teacher, attempting to educate the partner about what the partner did "wrong." The "lesson" (which is almost always being ignored by the partner, who is off in his or her own head preparing a defense) is usually closely followed by a justification of the person's own position and we can easily predict where it will all lead. We tell Allison we are, instead, looking for a simple expression of anger.

She is stopped cold. Angry though she is, she doesn't know where to go from this point. We suggest she bring out her anger without words. She waits for a minute or two. She says this is a really hard thing to do. Finally, she taps one of the pillows a few times and makes a peep. Gradually she starts to twist the pillow and make angry sounds but still she has a smile on her face (the good girl remains in control).

At this point Allison is going through the motions but is still not expressing her anger. However, she keeps at it a little longer and her face starts to become red. Anger begins to flash through her eyes but just as an angry feeling is about to be expressed, she breaks into tears. This is a typical sequence of events for women who are living in their immature emotional child. Perhaps she needs to experience these tears, but the main point here is that she is still not expressing her anger.

Dan, meanwhile, is sitting stoically, with what appears to be a slight grin on his face. He is not moving a muscle. We ask him what he is feeling while all this is going on with his partner. He says he is "feeling" curious. When pressed a little further to reveal his feelings, he says he "feels" as if he wants to help her. We point out that none of these responses is a feeling from within himself; we ask what *he* is feeling. He says he isn't feeling anything.

We go back to Allison, who appears to be dejected. In response to our inquiry, she says she felt a little relief at having expressed some anger but now feels sad. More than that, she feels hopeless. And lonely.

Over on Dan's side, there is some hopelessness, too. He now feels sad (a clue that he is probably more adept at feeling her feelings than his own). He says he feels like withdrawing.

We go back to Allison, who by this time is really beginning to feel angry! She is seeing him move into his old familiar patterns of behavior. First he wasn't feeling anything, which seems to her as if he was holding himself above her; now he withdraws like a little boy, just like he always does!

Her face is red. Her eyes are flashing. She lets out a shriek, goes after the pillows, and really lets her anger rip. No words, just the sounds and movement of anger energy. She goes on and on and finally rests for a moment. We ask her what she is feeling now. She says she is feeling a little better and adds that there is lots more to come. Then she lets loose again.

Dan is visibly startled by her expression of anger. We ask him what he is feeling. He feels "shaky." We ask him to look deeper into himself. He feels "agitation." What's that, exactly? we ask. He says he feels some fear, maybe mixed in with a little bit of excitement.

We go back to Allison. How is she feeling now? She feels alive, glad he feels fear and "a little bit of excitement." At least he is finally feeling *something*. After this last comment, we notice a shift in Dan.

So we ask Dan what he is now feeling. He senses she is looking down on him and says he is beginning to feel some anger. Okay, we ask, do you want to express any of that anger? Dan goes on to *explain* his response to her comment. This is not expression of anger as we define it and we know his rational analysis will only take him farther away from feelings. His discourse will only serve to invite more defensive responses from her.

We ask him if he is willing to express his anger without words. This time Dan is stumped. He says he is not feeling anger anymore (and he believes he isn't). From our point of view, though, we know anger is still present in him; he has now moved to a protective position, where he is denying his feelings.

We go to Allison, who was expectant but is beginning to drop into resignation as Dan waffles, backing away from his anger. What is she feeling now? She feels sad, disappointed, bored. She feels disgust. She still feels angry. She doesn't want anything to do with him. She wants to back away. She feels rejected.

Dan is surprised by the intensity of her response and wants to figure it out. We explain to him that we are at an essential difference between men and women. Words and rational understanding are his domain; feelings are hers. They have already tried plenty of words. If he wants to move through to deeper intimacy with her at this moment and avoid falling back into the peanut butter, he'll have to risk expressing a feeling.

He hears this as a demand and . . . feels angry. "Why does it always have to be her way? She always seems to be in control!" His anger is up again, so we suggest he might as well try expressing it.

Dan stops and looks around, as if to find a way out of this. He says he now understands what she meant when, at the beginning of this interchange, she said expressing anger was difficult. He now takes a breath and lets out a lion's roar. He pounds the pillows. He's forcing it at first but before long the anger he has been holding in all this time starts to break through. When it finally comes, it's a torrent.

After he is spent for the moment, we go back over to Allison and ask her what she is feeling. Allison feels some fear but more than that, she feels excited and, for lack of a better word, *happy*. She feels relieved. She feels affection. We go back over to Dan and discover he is nonplussed by her response. Why should she feel excited and happy at his raging? It is the exact opposite of what he expected. Nonetheless, when he goes inside himself, he discovers he is feeling relief and affection for Allison. At this moment, there is an opening for intimacy and we can begin.

Obviously, Allison and Dan have a long way to go yet. Huge amounts of anger still reside in both of them, anger that needs to be expressed. But once a start has been made with anger, we can easily predict that, with a little guidance to help keep them on track, they will discover many other emotions flooding forth as well. If this relationship still has some life in it and if honest feelings continue to be expressed, we can almost guarantee that passion, sexuality, and other feelings—more pleasing to both of them—will eventually emerge along with the anger.

WHAT CAN BE LEARNED FROM THIS EXCHANGE?

Expressing Angry Feelings Requires Vulnerability

Allison and Dan are typical of couples who come into our office with anger spilling out all over. Both are capable of delivering a long litany of complaints, grudges, and resentments, but when invited to express their feelings of anger without blaming words or long discourses on the partner's inadequacies, they actually become shy or withdrawn. Men often go totally blank. Women might come up with tears, sadness, or disappointment, but usually not anger. After a period of searching for angry feelings, the usual response from both men and women goes something like, "Well, I'm not feeling angry right this minute."

What they are really saying is that they are afraid of anger and would prefer to avoid expressing it, continuing instead with their old behavior patterns. Verbal combat is safer. Pointing out the other's faults or trying to teach the other about his or her wrong behavior is much easier. Assuming the critic or teacher role in relationship is essentially a safe, defensive posture. Partners in this role are able to hold themselves above the other and don't risk anything.

When we "took away" their usual strategies for showing anger and encouraged them to actually *express* it, clearly and directly, both had a great deal more difficulty. In order to express their feelings, they needed to come down out of their critic/blaming/teacher/controlling positions and participate in the relationship in a real way. They needed to move into themselves. Allison and Dan discovered that expressing feelings, even feelings like anger, requires vulnerability. (Interestingly, after they both let down their usual defensive posturing and allowed some of that type of vulnerability, feelings of affection began to emerge.)

Anger Needs to Be Received

One of the most important things that can be learned from the example of Allison and Dan is that anger needs to be *received* for it to enhance intimacy. Otherwise, it is essentially a narcissistic process. Yes, expression does provide some relief, but it only benefits the person who is expressing. However, anger that is voiced *and* received actually has the potential to be nourishing to both parties. How does this work?

As we saw in the session, the first time Allison expressed anger, Dan didn't receive it. At that moment, his response was that he felt "curious." However, one doesn't "feel" curious; one "thinks" curious. He was in his head and not his feelings. He was analyzing and judging her rather than being with her or receiving who she was at that moment.

His second response indicated that he wanted to help her. The desire to help another is an admirable quality. But when a partner proposes to help the other at a time when *both* are caught in a sticky situation, the helper is really taking a power position relative to the partner, who then becomes the "patient," with less power. The partner who is being "helped" in this way is not usually delighted about receiving it.

Dan's third perception was that he wasn't feeling anything as Allison expressed her anger. When people don't react to a potent expression of anger from their intimate partner, we know they are closed off and in defense. Any way you look at it, Dan was walled off against her feeling.

When Allison's expression of anger was not received by Dan, she went through a number of feelings. She felt a small amount of relief at having expressed some anger, though her predominant experience was of disappointment and loneliness. This is typical: a woman in relationship with a man who refuses to receive her anger ends up feeling hopeless and lonely.

The second time Allison expressed anger was different. This time Dan came up with a feeling when she got angry. The actual feelings he had are not as important as the fact that he felt *something* in response to her anger. He let go of some of his defense. He felt "shaky," which then got refined to feelings of "fear" and "excitement." The fact that he felt *something* was a sign to her that her feelings, her expression of herself, were at least partially received. His having received her feelings helped her to experience greater aliveness at that moment. Her feeling of aliveness and hope ultimately led to her having more affection for him

187

as the session progressed. The reason for this is simple: women feel nourished by emotions; when they feel nourished by their intimate partner, they want to nourish in return. We observe that a woman whose anger is not received ends up feeling hopeless and lonely, whereas a woman whose anger is received feels alive and ready to give of herself. (Even though this example deals with gender stereotypes, the situation obviously can occur in the reverse.)

When one partner alone generates a feeling, the effect is minuscule compared to what can happen when that feeling is received. Anger that is expressed and received involves the completion of a circuit, which permits life-energy to flow. Just like an electrical current, flowing life-energy (in this case, having started from anger) has the potential to be transformed and experienced in many ways, such as affection, sexuality, creativity, and zest for life. Feeding on this energy, both parties have an enhanced potential to become more aware and whole. Expressed anger that meets a stone wall or is only reflected back accumulates—and leads to yet more anger.

A Refusal to Express Anger Is a Rejection

When both partners refuse to express anger outright, you can almost be certain that a great deal of rejection exists underneath the surface of the relationship. It's quite the opposite of what we might think.

In order to see an example of how this works, we need to return to the point in the session when Dan's anger first poked through. Allison had said she was glad he felt some fear (shakiness) when she expressed anger. Then she gave him a little jab when she said she was glad he was "finally feeling *something*." If we were to put the microscope on Dan, we would probably notice that he started to feel some anger when he heard she was glad he felt fearful. Perhaps she was gaining the upper hand; perhaps she was gloating. When he heard her remark about his finally feeling something, his anger came to the surface. He "heard" her saying, in a sly kind of way, "You're still not doing it well enough."

But Dan's feeling of anger "disappeared" quickly. He went to words and started to engage in intellectual combat, a domain where he felt more competence. Essentially he was using his words to cover his feelings and to attempt re-establishing a sense of being in control. Naomi and I suggested he refrain from expressing himself in words (which we already knew he could do very well) and risk a direct expression of his anger. He went blank and reported that he felt nothing.

At this critical point, when Allison was asked to go inward, she reported feeling rejected. (And we could predict that without intervention, the next step for her would be to automatically—i.e., unconsciously—reject him in return, thus contributing to the vicious circle which brought them to therapy.) But the surprising question that pops up here is: why should *she* feel rejected because *he* denied his anger?

As Allison heard it, Dan's refusal to come out with his feelings (feelings she "knew" were there) was just another way of his saying "no" to her. She heard: "No, I won't face my anger . . . no, I won't tell you who I am and what is going on with me . . . no, I don't want intimacy with you . . . no, I won't risk going any deeper . . . no, I won't grow up." In addition to being disgusted by his little boy saying "no" all the time, she felt rejected in intimacy, *rejected as a woman*. No man was present for the woman part of her to relate with.

When this type of interaction happens in their everyday life, she is not aware of herself enough to articulate her responses. She just silently feels sadness, disgust, disappointment, and so on. She feels rejected and undernourished as a woman, but can't figure out why. She does sense she wouldn't be feeling this way if he would just come out with his feelings. Her solution is to press harder for them. As she presses harder, he interprets it as an attempt to control him. He doesn't want to feel controlled by her and continues to say "no" (like the little boy to his mother).

He denies rejecting her, perhaps even presenting himself as the nice guy. He puts forth a rational argument that he is not the angry one; if anyone is angry in the relationship, she is. But since *his words* don't

189

match *her feelings*, she begins to feel as if she must be crazy. She eventually withdraws and rejects him in return. He senses her rejection and becomes more defensive. On we go, down this switchback highway to a town called "Resignation."

This time, in the counseling session, Dan's and Allison's usual pattern of relating was interrupted somewhat. With a little coaching, she was able to articulate what she was feeling—as opposed to swallowing it or blaming him for not receiving her. He, with a little reminder to slow down, was able to receive what she said and not just go into his automatic habitual defense (the silent rejection). He was surprised by her response and wanted to go a little farther.

Dan wondered why she was experiencing rejection (and sadness, disgust, etc.). Why should *she* feel rejected? His mind went back into the past and he could remember plenty of times when *he* risked expressing a feeling and she was the one who rejected *him*. Why does *he* always seem to get the blame put on himself? *He* was disgusted by *her* controlling nature.

Dan's choice was to keep on attempting to figure this out or to express his feelings of the moment (which were indignation and anger). Naomi and I realized that his figuring-it-out would only be perceived by Allison as more rejection. We encouraged him to let go of figuring-it-out and express his anger directly. After a moment's hesitation, he did.

As Dan expressed his anger, Allison experienced a variety of feelings, but rejection and disgust weren't among them. Her eyes lit up. She felt excitement, relief, and affection. She felt excited because she saw his aliveness and felt vitalized by it. She felt relief because he was showing more than his defensive, emotionally young boy-part. She also felt relief because she had been thinking the relationship would fail if he stayed stuck behind his wall, and suddenly there was hope. She felt relieved of the burden of carrying all the anger in their relationship. She sensed he was bringing out his adult man, which allowed her to be more in her woman. She felt love for him.

We can see how this might be confusing for Dan (and most men). Dan learned a long way back in his life that the expression of anger means the risk of censure and rejection (the loss of love). Yet now, with his intimate partner, he finds the expression of angry feelings results in more aliveness. In earlier years, he was taught to hold back his anger to avoid being rejected. Now, with his intimate partner, he finds that when he holds back his anger, he *gets* rejected! Part of the problem for him is that he hasn't updated himself. The "good boy" might have worked with his mother but it won't work with his wife.

Partners Want Anger and They Don't

In our example with Allison and Dan, Allison was mostly able to receive Dan's anger when it came, but part of her was afraid. This is typical. In many sessions, we have seen situations where the woman says she wants feelings (including anger) from her partner, but when he rages, she collapses into fear or becomes defensive and controlling. In whatever way is familiar to her, she adopts a strategy intended to control or at least disarm his anger.

Her ambivalence is easier to understand if we separate out her adult woman from her inner, emotionally young girl. The woman part of her wants to have anger out in the open. She welcomes the true feelings, whatever they are. If he can bring out his anger, she feels more freedom to bring out her anger and not always be holding back. In this way, perhaps she will be able to develop her fuller feminine and give the outdated good girl a rest. In any case, the woman part of her knows she gets nourished by feelings, and anger will eventually lead to more aliveness.

However, the child part of her doesn't want his anger. The response of her emotionally young child to anger is tears, withdrawal, or defense. Anger is too threatening for her, too much to cope with. It has the potential to overwhelm her and the child part of her only wants to feel safe. The child part is looking for a gentle, supportive father and those types of men are not angry.

Once again, everything we say about one gender can and ought to be applied to the opposite gender at varying times and stages in a relationship. We've presented an example in which a woman wants and doesn't want anger, but the same holds for a man. He wants her juiciness and passion but he doesn't want her anger. The man part of him wants a powerful, feeling woman and the boy part of him doesn't want anything out of her that might threaten him.

Allison: "No man can be with my anger!"

Deep in her psyche, Allison—along with many other women— probably believes neither Dan nor any man would be able to be with her if she were to let her full power out. This belief is confirmed when the woman's partner—in this case, Dan—is evidently not able to match her in her feelings, to stand into expressing and receiving anger with her. The net result is that she secretly points the finger at him (and men in general) for being the reason she can't bring out her power (rather than looking inside herself, where the biggest problem exists). As Dan continues to avoid anger, her myth gets reinforced.

When Dan does express his anger, she can't just stay stuck, swallowing her own anger and power, using him and his "deficiencies" as an excuse. As he comes out, she is inspired to come out as well. She feels relief. Rather than her attitude being one of demeaning him, she feels more confidence in him as a man and begins to learn that she must look more into herself to bring out her own power.

Dan: "Why can't we just work things out rationally?"

Reasoning is a wonderful tool and a necessary skill, but we also need to recognize that Dan, along with just about every man, prefers to reason it out when things get hot because he prefers to play one of his stronger cards. If he can get his internal courtroom lawyer into the act, sooner or later he'll be able to work things around so she is proved to be wrong. In short, he uses words to gain an experience of power.

The woman on the receiving end of this "word power" often feels (justifiably) suspicious. Feelings are her strong suit and though she often gets pulled into rational arguments when he is disguising anger, things just don't feel right to her. His words might sound good but underneath, they "feel" deceptive and even passive-aggressive. In a slick way, he is using words to justify himself, to regain a sense of control, to put one over on her.

Neither reason nor feelings, when used exclusively to approach a relationship issue, will work (that's what makes everything so interesting and complex). Dan needs to recognize that he has overdeveloped his rational side and if he wants to avoid falling back into the peanut butter again in his relationship, he'll have to cut back the words and learn to express anger (or whatever he feels at the moment) directly.

The All-or-Nothing Dilemma

If we had carried on further with the interaction between Dan and Allison, we would almost certainly have come to a dilemma that most men experience in one form or another. I recall one man's succinct description. Referring to his hot-blooded partner, he said, "When she comes after me with her anger, I feel as though I'm facing a mad dog. My only choice is to come out full force or run away. If I came at her with full force, I might hurt her; since I don't want to hurt her, I run away." By this point he had already recognized that running away would only make her angrier, so it seemed like a no-win situation for him.

This type of all-or-nothing conceptualization is typical. This man was as afraid of his own anger as he was of his partner's. He didn't trust his own boundaries, and the unspoken issue was that he was actually afraid of being overpowered by his partner. The question he needed now to ask himself, at the midpoint in his life, was whether he had developed his boundaries and his mature, adult masculine sufficiently to be able to express anger without going over the edge into abuse. Was he so small inside that he would need to come out full force and attempt to vanquish his partner just to prove he could "win"?

The all-or-nothing conceptualization belongs more to the immature child part than it does to the mature adult.

Emotional Children Have Difficulty with Anger

Most families in our culture are not comfortable with anger. Though parents have lots of it, they aren't skilled in expressing it. That creates a confusing situation for the kids, who eventually learn that the way to feel safe is either to model after the parents (which only leads to a continuation of dysfunction with anger) or find ways to avoid the territory altogether.

Some children close down to the threat of anger by bringing up an internal emotional wall and closing off their vulnerability; some become collapsed and helpless; some learn to deflect the anger (with humor, for example); some decide to be perfect; a few learn to be aggressive and strike first. Whatever the strategy, the child learns to avoid expression of anger (as we have defined it), because the power of anger is too much to cope with.

The child also gets the idea that expressing anger is not acceptable behavior and means risking reprisal and the loss of love. Behaving or "being" in ways that will not risk reprisal is what's called for. If children want to feel safe, they learn that putting on a mask and swallowing their feelings is the better course.

As we have seen throughout this book, many individuals bring this same "child" with them into their intimate relationships. These internal children *still* do not have the resources to cope with the power of anger. To them, anger often signals the end of love. Thus, they want to control the manifestation of anger in the relationship and make things safe. A person who sleeps alone may be able to "transcend" (or at least become convinced that he or she has transcended) anger, but no person in an intimate relationship will be able to "transcend" it for long. Anger *will appear* and the person *will have to learn* how to deal with it! Partners must decide whether they will continue to allow these boring inner child parts to play a dominant role for the rest of their lives, or whether they will update themselves and learn to call upon other inner resources.

Mature adults in intimate relationship know that anger and love can both exist at the same time. When the mature masculine and feminine are present and a clean expression of anger occurs, truth often comes up that wouldn't emerge in any other way. Healthy boundaries can be renewed. Partners can be jolted off their selfish, egocentric positions.

A Refusal to Deal with Anger Can Be Costly

Every course of action has a cost. When anger is not expressed, it usually ends up being emitted in the form of frozen smiles, bickering, sarcasm, sulking, smoldering, contempt, rejection, or just plain indifference. Bodies and faces distort over the years. Passive-angry individuals are often quite unconscious of the ways they slowly torture those around them. Others repress their anger until they can't hold it anymore. At this point it explodes and comes out in unpredictable, potentially damaging ways. The person who holds it all in is not necessarily a safe person to be with.

HOMEWORK

Talking about the expression of anger in relationship is one thing; actually practicing it is another. A lifetime of habit does not disappear easily. After the hard work of *acknowledging* their own anger, partners must develop skills in expression and overcome habitually defensive reactions when anger appears in a partner. This is one arena where skilled therapeutic guidance can greatly accelerate positive movement.

For couples who are new to these ideas, we always recommend a daily "anger meditation"—especially for partners who habitually swallow their anger. After the distinction between expressing anger, emitting anger, and doing damage is clear, we suggest they make a commitment to find time and space each day for about ten to twenty minutes of anger expression on their own. They might hit a punching bag, chop wood, pound pillows, look in a mirror and bring out anger in their eyes, or do whatever they can to let anger out. If the environment allows it, expressing sounds heightens the experience.

The ultimate goal of these exercises is not to train two raving children how to have temper tantrums in each other's presence (although that may happen now and again). Anger meditations do serve to release bottled-up anger but, more important, they can assist couples to become more alert to their own inner feelings. Partners discover they can express what is going on inside without doing damage. They learn that expressing anger is a skill. By developing that skill, they begin to feel as if they have a resource they can use to deal with their partners in a more open way. They don't have to revert to passive, manipulative strategies based on hiding anger. As partners become more alert to themselves, they feel less need to project their own unresolved feelings onto the other person.

Once again, the consequences of not doing some homework on anger are not pretty. When anger is controlled, denied, or withheld in relationship, things may appear peaceful on the surface but partners eventually become tight and overcontrolled. Bottled-up anger goes underground. Sexuality is usually one of the first casualties because, despite what the "child" might like to believe, one cannot mask anger and still sustain passion. The health and well-being of the individuals is ultimately at stake, because anger that is not expressed outward often seems to get redirected inward, against the self.

12

RELATIONSHIP IS NOT FOR THE FEINT OF HEART

WHERE WE'VE BEEN

We began our journey together by examining the shadow side of partners in the early stages of relationship. We looked at how they enter into a type of silent collusion with each other to avoid dealing with conflict, anger, control, competition, judgment, rejection, and any of the darker (or shadow) parts that exist in all human beings. We saw that partners who avoid these parts end up playing roles and living behind masks. *Both* are stuck with an emotionally underdeveloped child: the one they're in relationship with and their own!

In the earlier stages, most partners opt to hide or deny shadow parts of themselves in their attempt to prolong "love" and avoid abandonment. Doing so makes life easier for the moment, but they pay a price. Partners who live in idealization and delusion about the difficult aspects in themselves eventually end up rejecting each other as the ordinary human beings they are. They find themselves investing their energy in trying to change their mate to coincide with their own vision of an ideal and then justifying the "rightness" of their position. As they do this, they get locked into struggles over control and power. The relationship eventually stagnates; they close off to each other. Anger increases as the prospect of being trapped in a dead situation looms. Their collusion to avoid difficulties in the relationship results in a diminishing love and in emotional abandonment—the very circumstances they were attempting to avoid.

Couples who don't proceed past the masking stage usually end up with a very limited repertoire of behavior patterns in their intimate relationship. They act out either a child role or a parent role. (The child role is actually closer to who they really are, though they don't want to see that, whereas the parent role is acted out as a defense against their immaturity.) Neither partner wants to see that they are each peers in terms of emotional age, so both attack the other for what they perceive the other lacks as an authentic adult man or adult woman.

Because both partners are so young internally, each feels as if the other somehow has control. Operating from this (unconscious) stance, they struggle all the harder to secure control and actually compete for it as though their life depended on it. Rather than looking at their own smallness and feelings of inadequacy, they try to bring their partner down—in hidden (and sometimes not so hidden) ways.

Both partners end up feeling undernourished and weakened by their intimate relationship instead of strengthened by it. As the immature part of a man refuses to come to terms with his own inner feelings, he unconsciously starves his partner by withholding that which she needs most to flourish. And he can't understand why she eventually refuses to nourish *him*. As the immature part of a woman refuses to receive her partner and quietly disparages him, he doesn't get the support he needs. And she can't understand why he seems unable to give her the nourishment she needs.

All this makes for a fascinating dance, because the partners are not conscious of their own roles and yet both play their parts with great enthusiasm. Without awareness of their own respective contributions, the partners find themselves mysteriously unfulfilled. Emotionally young women who are seeking out the powerful, supportive, adult masculine are disappointed when they repeatedly realize they have a defended, emotionally immature parent-boy for a mate. At the same time, emotionally young men are seeking out the passionate, receptive adult feminine and don't know what to do with the needy, controlling parent-girl who emerges after the romantic stage.

The partners do not really know who they are as individuals or what they feel underneath the surface. Both want to live in a child's idealistic world, with themselves as hero. Blaming gets directed at the partner when difficulties arise. A lot of this stays hidden because the partners do not want to acknowledge openly how small and blaming they feel. A huge amount of anger exists below the surface, but neither person is able to cope with directly expressing and/or receiving it.

In a stalemated situation, both partners are defended and want to think they know best. Little inspiration exists for developing personal awareness. They are focused outward to see what is wrong with their mate but are not willing to look honestly at themselves and how their roles contribute to the deadness. Both partners find themselves blocked from developing their adult masculine and feminine. Surrendering is out of the question, even over the most minor issues. From the "no surrender" position, both individuals end up even more emotionally starved and cut off from the opportunity to have their needs met.

Then, as their marriage is beginning to show signs of not living up to the ideal . . . a child is born. They do not have the capacity to be real parents; they are emotional children playing the role of parents. Not knowing how to parent authentically, they either abandon the child emotionally or overbond with it (in the name of love). Whichever course they take, the child is powerfully affected by the charade. The parents, unless they wake up to themselves, invariably end up passing along the legacy of dysfunction in intimacy. Years later, their children turn out to be as dysfunctional in intimacy as the parents are.

WHERE WE'RE GOING

A response Naomi and I frequently receive after presenting this material is that individuals are discouraged and perhaps even feel despair about experiencing ongoing, fulfilling intimacy. Now that they recognize a few of the stuck spots, they feel overwhelmed at the prospect of altering what's going on. If they have confidence in their own ability to change, they have difficulty seeing their partners as willing to grow. They ask us what can be done to make their relationship more nourishing and functional in an ongoing way.

The basic truth is that enhanced, sustained intimacy requires significantly expanded awareness in both partners. Both need to grow up into more mature beings. But how does one expand one's own awareness and grow when one is stuck?

Partners Need to Grow Each Other Up

A couple really only has one choice if they are to mature and discover more enriching possibilities with each other: *they need to grow each other up.* For whatever reason, their own parents were not fully up to the task and now they need to complete the job together. Only if they are successful in this project will they, in turn, have any hope of raising their kids to be emotional adults, thus breaking this cycle of dysfunction in intimacy.

Restating the dilemma: the son part of a man is not really capable of matching and supporting the woman he is with. Without his support and challenge, she gets stuck in playing out an emotionally young role. The daughter part of a woman is not capable of authentically nourishing and challenging the man she is with. Without her mature feminine, he gets stuck playing out an emotionally young role.

How can this growing-each-other-up process turn into a cooperative effort between two individuals on one of life's most important quests, as opposed to a power struggle between two individuals who are each blinded to their inner being?

In order to begin waking up, a couple needs to be willing to uncover feelings and parts of themselves they would rather avoid. The partners must come to terms with their anger. They must get to know their neediness, along with the pain and despair of not having a real sense of self. Partners must move out of their "victim" posture and recognize how controlling each of them is.

This is sour medicine. Neither partner really wants to learn these lessons. Recognizing that they have a large inner part which is so emotionally young and is still looking for an ideal mother or father is something most people would rather not do—especially when their chronological age is moving into the forty-or-greater range! Unfortunately there is no other way to become authentic. We have to recognize where we are at this very moment, and do so *before* we can proceed in a truthful way in our intimate lives.

Men have to go deep inside themselves and honestly ask whether they want a daughter/mother or are up to supporting the development of a woman who will, at times, be more powerful than they are. Similarly, women have to keep on asking themselves (moment by moment, if necessary) whether they want a son/father or are truly willing to support the development of the powerful man they say they want.

Only Committed Partners Can Succeed

It takes two to dance the dance. Usually when a relationship isn't functioning as well as it should, at least one of the partners, whether that partner wants to admit it or not, has one foot out the door emotionally. Deep down, that person would probably rather live in fantasy and doesn't have the courage to leave. Partners in this position might think they are hiding it, but their mates always feel it one way or another. They feel rejected; they feel as if they are on trial; they feel danger in allowing vulnerability. Their defenses need to be on alert. Perhaps, deep down and unknowingly, they have decided that if their partner isn't "in," they aren't going to be the vulnerable one and risk being rejected.

In this type of situation, no technique, no strategy, no romantic spark is going to help the relationship function at a higher level. Partners first need to take a brutally clear look at whether they want to be "in" or not, whether they are willing to take that leap of faith. Until the clear decision to commit themselves is made, the couple will probably not put the required energy into their relationship, except during crises. And that won't be enough.

Both Partners Need to "Get a Self"

Individuals in a troubled relationship are almost invariably out of themselves, focusing on the other. Ordinarily in this situation, the man habitually looks to women to define himself and the woman has a history of using her relationships with men to do likewise. Underneath it all, each is looking for the other to provide the definition of the relationship—and thus is primed to blame the other when things don't go right.

Individuals who don't know themselves may function all right in short-term relationships but don't seem to have the "fire" that is required to sustain intimate relating, to keep a relationship passionate. Where does this fire come from? For Naomi and me, it came when we reached the point in our lives where we couldn't be satisfied with less. We were sufficiently uncomfortable with life as it was to be able to generate the determination to change things, to be more truthful, to keep up the energy that is required in a growing relationship.

In this book, though we've done our best to make you, the reader, uncomfortable with the status quo, the fuel for change needs to come from within you. If you do have that fuel, what are some basic, practical steps you can take to begin working on developing a self in relationship?

1. When things get difficult, don't run. Learn to observe when you are withholding yourself, becoming defensive, or preparing to attack. Try admitting it openly when you find yourself doing so. At the beginning, changing your behavior is not as important as becoming conscious of it at the moment it is happening—and speaking it out

202

assists with that. Remember, whether you withhold or attack, both reactions do violence to the relationship.

2. Keep asking yourself if you are in your head or your body. If you can become aware of your body, you are more present. If you are only in your head, figuring things out, the chances are that you are in defense and (unconsciously) looking for a way to get control.

3. Listen to your partner. If you have a history of not listening, repeat what you heard until your partner acknowledges that you have received the message he or she is trying to deliver. Watch for your tendency to *interpret* what was said rather than *repeating* what was said. When tensions are high, interpreting a partner is very close to controlling the partner, and controlling will get nowhere.

4. As you digest your partner's message, locate yourself again. If you are in your head, see if you can relocate into your body. What are you feeling? *Take the time* to go inward and find out. Allow yourself some room for imperfection; this is a new skill you are trying to develop.

5. Express what you are *feeling*. If you come out with something like, "I feel that . . . , " followed by an opinion, idea, or thought, catch yourself, because you are not feeling. You are in your head, about to deliver a discourse. Go back and see if you can come forth with, "I feel . . . , " and have the word that follows *actually be feeling-related*. If that next word does not have to do with a feeling, stop and try again. Watch to make sure the words that follow the feeling-word are directly related to a feeling and are not some kind of articulate avoidance.[*]

---

[*] This step is much easier to read about than to do. Be sure to allow yourself whatever time is required to come up with appropriate feeling-words and do it as truthfully as you can. Also be aware that people who smoke or addictively injest any other substance are likely to have extra difficulty locating and exposing their deeper feelings. Partners who genuinely want to practice this kind of work might experiment for a couple of weeks with quitting whatever substance they use and working with the discomforting feelings that exist underneath the smokescreen.

6.   Wait for your partner to hear you. If you question whether your partner heard you or not, ask him or her to repeat what you said. Allow your partner time to feel his or her feelings in response to what you just said.

7.   Ask for your partner's feelings. Observe whether what you get is expressing a feeling or is from the person's intellect.

8.   Go back and forth in this format until some clarity emerges. Have patience. You may not be able to locate the precise feelings until sometime after the fact, but if you have the perseverance to stay working with this approach, the time-delay will shorten.

9.   Follow up with: "What do you need?" When "I don't know" comes up, encourage your partner to dig a little deeper.

10.   Listen again. Watch your response. You may not be able to deliver what is needed at the moment; the most important thing is that the partner is heard.

11.   Look into yourself and express what you feel you need. Take a risk and try expressing it. You can never tell what might happen.

The Necessity for Vulnerability

—It takes a lot of guts to expose feelings.

—It takes guts to see oneself as flawed and immature.

—It takes guts to recognize feelings of powerlessness in the presence of your intimate partner.

—It takes guts to deal with anger head-on.

Awareness must expand, and expansion of awareness cannot happen without *vulnerability*. Undernourished partners with a history of frustration, defense, and blaming do not have an easy time allowing themselves to be vulnerable, especially in the presence of the other. Yet, once again, their relationship isn't going anywhere unless they are willing to humble themselves enough to acknowledge that they have major blind spots in their own being, and that neither is as aware as they might "think" they are.

Paradoxically, a couple who discovers that neither is, at the moment, sufficiently aware has already jumped over one of the most difficult hurdles. The idea that they share *equal* responsibility for any dysfunction in their relationship soon follows. It slowly dawns that movement in a relationship will only occur and can only be sustained when both partners are willing to move in equal proportion. They begin to realize that when they take a step forward in their relationship, they take a step in their own maturity and wisdom.

THE IMPORTANCE OF FEELINGS

The single most important way to enhance a relationship over the long run is through *learning to express and receive feelings.* When both individuals are able to contact their feelings, share them with each other, and have them received, awareness of *what is really happening* will emerge. From what we have seen, when two partners get to know who they really are and learn to accept each other as they are, deeper intimacy and love follow.

Easily said—but how do two people who are, in large part, blind to their feelings, who have spent a lifetime covering them over, suddenly start communicating on this level? We've listed just a few steps to help individuals in relationship begin learning to locate, express, and receive feelings. Determined individuals can make a lot of progress if they are willing to follow these steps. It is also true that training oneself to become more aware on the feeling levels is a skill that is not easily learned without some kind of objective outside help. All of us are too subject to our own delusions about ourselves. Few of us received adequate modeling and training at the earlier stages of life, so long-standing habits are in the way. At first, partners who are stalemated have difficulty listening and thus receiving this help from each other. Awareness of feelings is new, unfamiliar territory and partners usually need to find someone whose guidance and input they value.

In our experience, learning to express and receive feelings, learning to locate self in relationship, comes most easily when the process is witnessed and then experienced. We have found that the fastest and most effective way of learning these skills takes place in facilitated groups. And couples move most quickly when they are with their partner in a group with other couples. For a summary of some fundamental aspects of couples' groups, see Appendix B.

THE END OF OUR JOURNEY

We started our journey with the image of partners dancing in the dark, unable to see their way to a more fulfilling relationship. Both were frustrated and stuck, unwilling to look at their own contribution to their difficulties together. Now, as we conclude, we are able to recognize that instead of escaping from the "darkness," their going *into* it is a direct avenue to truth, awareness, and a juicy relationship.

Naomi and I have found that dancing in the dark with each other (and the couples we work with) has helped us become more aware and whole as individuals. It's a process of uncovering pieces of ourselves bit by bit—all the inner characters that have been mentioned in this book. In actuality, while working on these issues is much easier talked about than done, bringing awareness to unconscious patterns and attempting to live in the truth of one's feelings is exhilarating work. It creates the possibility of sustaining a passion in relationship that, ultimately, far surpasses the transitory affection of romantic love.

A major part of the human experience is to be continually developing in self-awareness. As each new layer of awareness emerges, an opportunity appears for us to develop an even deeper self-acceptance. As we develop broader awareness and self-acceptance, we begin to experience wholeness and wellness. And as this occurs, we build a foundation that permits us to move from the egocentric child to the fully empowered adult.

Doing it together in intimate relationship can be one of life's great opportunities or one of life's biggest headaches. The choice is yours. Happy dancing!

APPENDIX A

A Note about Subpersonalities

Most of us would prefer to believe we are just one coherent self, with one inner identity, operating in one body. Then life would be so much simpler, so much more consistent and rational. (It might also be dull to the point of being unbearable!)

But the reality is that we are *not* one single, coherent self, and we are filled with a jumble of conflicting inner characters, each with their individual voices, feelings, urges, thoughts. Psychotherapists have learned that one way to better understand the complexities of the self is to unscramble that jumble by assigning to each of the major inner voices an identity of its own. Once an inner voice has been identified, it can be isolated from other inner voices and examined. Some psychotherapists, including ourselves, use the term "subpersonalities" to describe these voices, or partial identities.

As Naomi and I see it, each person is made up of a stew of many subpersonalities, or inner characters. Though each person's particular recipe is different, we believe each person, somewhere within, has access to every subpersonality in the human drama. Some of these inner characters stand out more than others and an individual's overall personality depends on which ones tend to be prominent. People accept and value some of their subpersonalities; they reject and do not value others, usually because those particular subpersonalities do not enhance the vision they want to hold of themselves. For obvious reasons, the unenhancing ones are usually the ones that attract therapeutic attention.

The inner human drama becomes even more fascinating when one discovers that each prominent, easily-seen part also has an opposite, invisible aspect lurking beneath conscious awareness. Together, these hidden aspects contribute to a part of self that is often referred to as one's *shadow*. For example, the person who is noticeably self-effacing has a shadow subpersonality who is arrogant. Or the person who shows great strength and power on the surface has a subpersonality who feels impotent. Someone noted for generosity will find a stingy subpersonality lurking in the shadow.

In looking at the subpersonalities which tend to be most evident between intimate partners, we find that every woman has a mother part, a daughter part, and an adult mature woman part. Similarly, every man has a father part, a son part, and an adult mature man part. (To make it even more rich and complex, every man also has feminine parts and each woman has masculine parts.)

As we have explained at length in the main text, we believe awareness, truth, and wholeness can be greatly facilitated by getting to know one's major subpersonalities—including those that exist in the shadow side of self. With regard to relationship, breaking things down into subpersonalities and learning to recognize which character is on stage at any given moment can add immeasurably to the understanding of complex patterns of behavior that emerge as things progress in the relationship. Awarenesses are possible that are not available when a person insists that a human being can be described only in terms of one, individual, complete adult person.

For readers who would like to explore the multidimensional models of human personality a little further, we recommend *Embracing Our Selves*[*] or one of the many texts on a school of psychotherapy called Psychosynthesis.

---

[*] *Embracing Our Selves* by Hal Stone, Ph.D., and Sidra Winkelman, Ph.D. (Devorss & Co., Marina del Rey, CA. 1985).

APPENDIX B

Couples' Groups

Most couples who are in a knot tend to view their own situation as uniquely complex and difficult. They feel alone; everyone else seems to be doing okay. They are usually reluctant to seek help because they believe they somehow shouldn't be having the difficulties they are having. Even when they do seek counseling, they frequently find that dysfunctional behavior patterns overpower them when they are alone together again.

From what Naomi and I have seen, couples need other couples who are willing to be honest in order to get the best perspective on themselves (and ultimately bring about enduring change). To deal effectively with a dysfunctional behavior pattern, a couple needs to work with it in a conscious way at the moment it is activated. But, when such a pattern is active, both partners are unconscious of their own roles and can't really see what is going on. In a couples' group, dysfunctional behavior patterns are invariably acted out in front of group members. In a properly facilitated group, couples have an opportunity to work things through at the moment they are happening, rather than just talking about the problems.

Couples who are observing other couples caught in dysfunctional patterns can discover things about themselves they just can't see when they, themselves, are acting out the patterns. Nothing will activate increased awareness quite like witnessing another emotionally blocked couple passionately speak the lines you and your partner usually speak. Once you become conscious in this way, blaming your partner for the difficulties in your relationship becomes harder and harder.

The truth is that the same basic issues are common to most couples and when partners share honestly in a group, this starts to become more evident. Couples in a group also go through a similar progression of experiences as the time they spend together increases. Thus, at the beginning of the group, partners are guarded, somewhat defensive, and trying to put on a happy face—which is just what they do in their own relationship. However, as they begin to get more honest, stored resentments and angry feelings emerge. They discover things about power and control struggles. As one couple risks exposing their issues, other couples are inspired to risk exposing *their* truths. Partners begin to see common threads running through all the relationships and feel less isolated.

In our own seminars, Naomi and I teach ways to recognize the mother/daughter/father/son parts. We cover other common problems—frequently using examples from our own relating patterns. As understanding increases, there is some relief. Partners feel a little freer to breathe.

Intellectual understanding needs to be balanced by training in feelings. High on the list is learning to deal with anger. In our work, we find ways to locate and express anger. We teach about the importance of receiving anger as well as expressing it. Once couples are less afraid of anger, things open up even more. There is relief.

Masks begin to let down. More truth comes out. Partners start to respect each other again. More feelings come out, some of which are not easy to expose. Even though some things might be difficult to receive, partners know when they are hearing truth, and they appreciate it. There is more relief. Partners begin to feel some excitement and even passion.

There is a recognition that they have been sexually closed. Resentments come up about that. More anger is expressed. Other specific issues surface. Couples learn that resolution is not nearly as important as having things out in the open, having one's viewpoint heard and acknowledged by the other. And on it goes.

Eventually everyone recognizes that each couple and each individual has something important to offer the group as a whole. Group members act as witnesses who can add clarity. Collective viewpoints can help break the loops of dysfunctional patterning that repeat over and over again in the absence of outside intervention. Participants recognize an opportunity to combine knowledge and get through to a new place.

At times, what becomes clear is that a relationship needs to end. But for the great majority, love and affection emerge in a stronger way. When both partners are feeling affection and nourishment, the desire to commit to each other in a deeper way follows naturally.

By the end of the group experience, couples express fear that they will fall back when they are on their own again. It is a well-justified fear, because we have seen that many couples retreat into old patterns of behavior about three or four weeks after a group ends. Enduring change needs some kind of follow-up support. Instituting new behavior patterns takes time.

Time is required to created a trusting environment where partners are willing to surrender to each other. Skills take time to be developed. Partners are also much more likely to stay alert to themselves when they realize they have made a commitment to report back to the group at a later point.

One effective group design we have found involves the same group of five to eight couples meeting and doing intense, feeling-oriented work three times over the course of about three months. Meetings are two weekend days in length, about a month apart. Naomi and I facilitate the weekends, and couples who are very enthusiastic might also meet, in a focused way, an extra weekday evening without us. We have seen positive, lasting changes in couples who have committed to this type of process.

Another very effective way to bring about positive changes for couples is in a residential retreat setting, where food and lodging are provided over the course of at least four days. When group members are separated from their day-to-day life, honesty and openness emerge more quickly. With the heightened intensity of the retreat environment, things move faster. With everything in the outer world cared for, partners have more opportunity to take a good look at themselves and reconnect with each other.

Whatever form it takes or however you go about doing it, don't be afraid to seek help.

INDEX

Psychosynthesis, 208

Relationship
  as a dance, 3
  commitment and, 201
  common problems summarized,
    197
  couples' groups, 209
  and feelings, 205
  "growing each other up," 200
  need for vulnerability, 204
  need to "get a self," 202
  sustaining intimacy in, 200–06
Romantic love. *See:* Love, romantic

Self, aspects of (subpersonalities)
  bitch/bastard, 21
  controller, 21
  good boy, 23
  good girl, 23
  in relationship, 3
  judge, 21
  punisher/dominator, 21
  seducer, 23
  user/abuser, 21
  victimizer, 21
Sex
  and anger, 175
  and blame, 163
  and commitment, 173
  in a committed relationship, 157

control vs. surrender, 169
difficulties with, 158
and egocentric partner, 160
enhancing in relationship, 168
and expectations, 162
immature partner and, 166
"meat-and-potatoes type," 174
not for "children," 166
rejection and, 160
role of in relationship, 178
struggle for power and control, 164
telling the truth and, 168
and touch, 172
Sexual abuse, overbonding as, 148
Sexual relating, "nuts & bolts" of,
  171
Shadow. *See also:* Dark side, the
  subpersonalities and, 208
Son type, 73–77
  and control, 109–18, 122–24
  as "father," 113
  evolution of, 123
  shadow side of, 75
Subpersonalities. *See also:* Self, aspects of
  defined, 207
  examples of, 4

Teacher, partner as, 125
Therapeutic assistance, need for, 130

Douglas and Naomi Moseley currently conduct workshops for couples and individuals in Taos, New Mexico, and at their retreat center in the mountains of British Columbia. In addition, they present lectures and seminars and offer retreats in other parts of the U.S. and Canada. For information about their schedule, contact them at:

216M Pueblo Norte #425
Taos, NM 87571
(505) 776-1074